Co

Ministry

Colporteur
Ministry

E. G. White

British Library Cataloguing in Publication Data
A catalogue record for this book is available from the British Library

This edition published by The Stanborough Press Ltd
Alma Park, Grantham, Lincs, NG31 9SL, England
Copyright © 2011

Cover design by David Bell

Printed in Thailand

ISBN 978-1-907456-08-4

Stanborough Press Ltd
United Kingdom

Foreword

Responding to a divine commission, Seventh-day Adventists have entered enthusiastically upon the work of heralding through the printed page the truths of the Sabbath and the Second Advent. In the more than a century of our evangelistic activity the publishing work has been a powerful agency for the spreading of the third angel's message around the world.

Through the years, guidance in publishing and circulating our literature has been given through the pen of Ellen G. White. In these counsels the selling of our truth-filled books and papers is elevated to a work comparable to that of the Gospel ministry. The seller of books is seen as a colporteur evangelist.

In 1902 a number of statements from the pen of Mrs. White relating to our colporteur ministry were assembled and published in a manual for canvassers. Subsequent Ellen G. White counsels on our literature ministry led to an enlargement of this work, and in 1920 the much loved *Colporteur Evangelist* appeared. This little work has been published in many languages and has been widely circulated.

The desire to eliminate repetition of subject matter, to place the counsels in a well-organized topical arrangement, and to include a few additional choice statements from the Ellen G. White books, periodical articles and manuscript files has led to this present compilation, which has been prepared in harmony with the provision established by Mrs. White for the posthumous publication of her writings. Reference is given for each quotation, and the year of writing or of first publication is noted.

Sideheads, supplied by the compilers, serve as an aid to the reader in finding desired statements. bold-faced type is used to introduce each excerpt, while italics are used for a heading within the statement itself. Except for a few statements, repetitious in character, the full content of Colporteur Evangelist is included in this new volume. All references are to original sources and not to Colporteur Evangelist, as it, too, was compiled after Mrs. White's death.

The reader will frequently find throughout the book such terms as 'canvassers,' 'tract and missionary society,' and 'canvassing agents.' These were the terms used in the times of Ellen G. White, and they will be readily understood by the reader.

That the counsels concerning literature evangelism, rearranged in this enlarged form, may guide and inspire colporteur evangelists to a richer and more effective ministry for the Master, is the sincere wish of the publishers and of

The trustees of the
Ellen G. White publications.

The bracketed numbers at the foot of each page co-ordinate this edition with the pagination of the standard hardback printings.

Contents

Section V
Our truth-filled literature

Section I

Colporteur evangelism

CHAPTER 1

Our literature and its mission

'Begin to Print.' – At a meeting held in Dorchester, Massachusetts, November, 1848, I had been given a view of the proclamation of the sealing message, and of the duty of the brethren to publish the light that was shining upon our pathway.

After coming out of vision, I said to my husband: 'I have a message for you. You must begin to print a little paper and send it out to the people. Let it be small at first; but as the people read, they will send you means with which to print, and it will be a success from the first. From this small beginning it was shown to me to be like streams of light that went clear round the world.' – *Life Sketches*, p. 125. (1915)

Make Truth Clear and Plain. – Our publications have a most sacred work to do in making clear, simple, and plain the spiritual basis of our faith. Everywhere the people are taking sides; all are ranging themselves either under the banner of truth and righteousness or under the banner of the apostate powers that are contending for the supremacy. At this time God's message to the world is to be given with such prominence and power that the people will be brought face to face, mind to mind, heart to heart, with truth. They must be brought to see its superiority over the multitudinous errors that are pushing their way into notice, to supplant, if possible, the word of God for this solemn time.

The great object of our publications is to exalt God, to call men's attention to the living truths of His word. God calls upon us to lift up, not our own standard, not the standard of this world, but His standard of truth. – *Testimonies*, vol. 7, pp. 150, 151. (1902)

Publish Light and Truth. – In the night of March 2, 1907, many things were revealed to me regarding the value of our publications on present truth and the small effort that is being made by our brethren and sisters in the churches for their wide circulation.

I have been repeatedly shown that our presses should now be constantly employed in publishing light and truth. This is a time of spiritual darkness in the churches of the world. Ignorance of divine things has hidden God and the truth from view. The forces of evil are gathering in strength. Satan flatters his co-workers that he will do a work that will captivate the world. While partial inactivity has come upon the church, Satan and his hosts are intensely active. The professed Christian churches are not converting the world; for they are themselves corrupted with selfishness and pride, and need to feel the converting power of God in their midst before they can lead others to a purer or higher standard. – *Testimonies*, vol. 9, p. 65. (1909)

Means of Quickly Giving the Message. – The book work should be the means of quickly giving the sacred light of present truth to the world. The publications that come forth from our presses today are to be of such a character as to strengthen every pin and pillar of the faith that was established by the word of God and by the revelations of His Spirit.

The truth that God has given for His people in these last days should keep them firm when there come into the church those who present false theories. The truth that has stood firm against the attacks of the enemy for more than half a century must still be the confidence and comfort of God's people.

Our evidence to nonprofessors that we have the truth of the word of God will be given in a life of strict self-denial. We must not make a mockery of our faith, but ever keep before us the example of Him who, though He was the Prince of heaven, stooped to a life of self-denial and sacrifice to vindicate the righteousness of His Father's word. Let us each resolve to do our best, that the light of our good works may shine forth to the world. – *Testimonies*, vol. 9, pp. 69, 70. (1909)

To Prepare a People to Meet God. – The publications sent forth from our printing houses are to prepare a people to meet God. Throughout the world they are to do the same work that was done by John the Baptist for the Jewish nation. By startling messages of warning, God's prophet awakened men from worldly dreaming. Through him God called backsliding Israel to repentance. By his presentation of truth he exposed popular delusions. In contrast with the false theories of his time, truth in his teaching stood forth as an eternal certainty. 'Repent ye: for the kingdom of heaven is at hand,' was John's message. Matthew 3:2. This same message, through the publications from our printing houses, is to be given to the world today. . . .

And in a large degree through our publishing houses is to be accomplished the work of that other angel who comes down from heaven with great power and who lightens the earth with his glory. – *Testimonies*, vol 7, pp. 139, 140. (1902)

Publications to Go Everywhere. – Our publications should go everywhere. Let them be issued in many languages. The third angel's message is to be given through this medium and through the living teacher. You who believe the truth for this time, wake up. It is your duty now to bring in all the means possible to help those who understand the truth to proclaim it. Part of the money that comes in from the sale of our publications should be used to increase our facilities for the production of more literature that will open blind eyes and break up the fallow ground of the heart. – *Testimonies*, vol. 9, p. 62. (1909)

There are many places in which the voice of the minister cannot be heard, places which can be reached only by our publications, – the books, papers, and tracts filled with the Bible truths that the people need. Our literature is to be distributed everywhere. The truth is to be sown beside all waters; for we know not which will prosper, this, or that. In our erring judgment we may think it unwise to give literature to the very ones who would accept the truth the most readily. We know not what may be the results of giving away a leaflet containing present truth. – *Manuscript* 127, 1909.

We are fast approaching the end. The printing and circulation of the books and papers that contain the truth for this time are to be our work. – *Testimonies*, vol. 8, p. 89. (1904)

To Every Country and Clime. – Publications must be multiplied, and scattered like the leaves of autumn. These silent messengers are enlightening and molding the minds of thousands in every country and in every clime. – *Review and Herald*, Nov. 21, 1878.

In Every Language. – From city to city, from country to country, they [canvasser-evangelists] are to carry the publications containing the promise of the Saviour's soon coming. These publications are to be translated into every language, for to all the world the gospel is to be preached. To every worker Christ promises the divine efficiency that will make his labors a success. – *Testimonies*, vol. 9, p. 34. (1909)

To Lighten the Whole World. – The world is to receive the light of truth through an evangelizing ministry of the word in our books and periodicals. – *Testimonies*, vol. 9, p. 61. (1909)

From our books and papers bright beams of light are to shine forth to enlighten the world in regard to present truth. – *Testimonies*, vol. 8, p. 87. (1904)

CHAPTER 2

A work second to none

Successful Soul-Saving Ministry. – The canvassing work, properly conducted, is missionary work of the highest order, and it is as good and successful a method as can be employed for placing before the people the important truths for this time. The importance of the work of the ministry is unmistakable; but many who are hungry for the bread of life have not the privilege of hearing the word from God's delegated preachers. For this reason it is essential that our publications be widely circulated. Thus the message will go where the living preacher cannot go, and the attention of many will be called to the important events connected with the closing scenes of this world's history.

A Work Ordained of God. – God has ordained the canvassing work as a means of presenting before the people the light contained in our books, and canvassers should be impressed with the importance of bringing before the world as fast as possible the books necessary for their spiritual education and enlightenment. This is the very work the Lord would have His people do at this time. All who consecrate themselves to God to work as canvassers are assisting to give the last message of warning to the world. We cannot too highly estimate this work; for were it not for the efforts of the canvasser, many would never hear the warning. – *Testimonies*, vol. 6, p. 313. (1900)

A Most Important Work. – If there is one work more important than another, it is that of getting our publications before the public, thus leading them to search the Scriptures. Missionary work – introducing our publications into families, conversing, and praying with and for them – is a good work and one which will educate men and women to do pastoral labor. – *Testimonies*, vol. 4, p. 390. (1880) When church members realize the importance of the circulation of our literature, they will devote more time to this work. Papers, tracts, and books will be placed in the homes of the people, to preach the gospel in their several lines. . . . The church must give her attention to the canvassing work. This is one way in which she is to shine in the world. Then will she go forth 'fair as the moon, clear as the sun, and terrible as an army with banners.' – *Manuscript* 113, 1901.

A Call for Revived Interest. – The importance of the canvassing work is kept ever before me. This work has not of late had the life infused into it which was once given by the agents who made it their specialty. Canvassers have been called from their evangelistic work to engage in other labor. This is not as it should be. Many of our canvassers, if truly converted and consecrated, can accomplish more in this line than in any other in bringing the truth for this time before the people.

We have the word of God to show that the end is near. The world is to be warned, and as never before we are to be laborers with Christ. The work of warning has been entrusted to us. We are to be channels of light to the world, imparting to others the light we receive from the great Light Bearer. The words and works of all men are to be tried. Let us not be backward now. That which is to be done in warning the world must be done without delay. Let not the canvassing work be left to languish. Let the books containing the light on present truth be placed before as many as possible. – *Testimonies*, vol. 6, p. 329. (1900)

Equal in Importance to the Ministry. – Canvassers must go out into various parts of the country. The importance of this work is fully equal to that of the ministry. The living preacher and the silent messenger are both required for the accomplishment of the great work before us. – *Review and Herald*, April 1, 1880.

Canvassing for our publications is an important and most profitable line of evangelistic work. Our publications can go to places where meetings cannot be held. In such places the faithful evangelistic canvasser takes the place of the living preacher. By the canvassing work the truth is presented to thousands who otherwise would never hear it. – *Review and Herald*, Oct. 7, 1902.

We have no time to lose. Important work is before us, and if we are slothful servants we shall certainly lose the heavenly reward. But few have broad and extensive views of what can be done in reaching the people by personal, interested efforts in a wise distribution of our publications. Many who will not be induced to listen to the truth presented by the living preacher will take up a tract or a paper and peruse it; many things they read meet their ideas exactly, and they become interested to read all it contains. – *Review and Herald*, Dec. 19, 1878.

To Understand Our Responsibility. – There is danger of entering into commercialism and becoming so engrossed in worldly business that the truths of the word of God in their purity and power will not be brought into the life. The love of trade and gain is becoming more and more prevalent. My brethren, let your souls be truly converted. If ever there was a time when we needed to understand our responsibilities, it is now, when truth is fallen in the streets and equity cannot enter. Satan has come down with great power to work with all deceivableness of unrighteousness in them that perish; and everything that can be shaken will be shaken, and those things that cannot be shaken will remain. The Lord is coming very soon, and we are entering into scenes of calamity. Satanic agencies, though unseen, are working to destroy human life. But if our life is hid with Christ in God, we shall see of His grace and salvation. Christ is coming to establish His kingdom on the earth. Let our tongues be sanctified and used to glorify Him. Let us work now as we have never worked before. We are exhorted to 'be instant in season, out of season.' 2 Timothy 4:2. We are to make openings for the presentation of the truth. We are to improve every opportunity of drawing souls to Christ.

As a people we are to be reconverted, our lives sanctified to declare the truth as it is in Jesus. In the work of scattering our publications, we can speak of a Saviour's love from a warm and throbbing heart. God alone has the power to forgive sins; if we do not speak this message to the unconverted, our neglect may prove their ruin. . . . The Lord calls upon all of us to seek to save perishing souls. Satan is at work to deceive the very elect, and now is our time to work with vigilance. Our books and papers are to be brought before the notice of the people; the gospel of present truth is to be given to our cities without delay. Shall we not arouse to our duties? – Testimonies, vol. 9, pp. 62, 63. (1909)

The Work of God. – Let the canvasser remember that he has an opportunity to sow beside all waters. Let him remember, as he sells the books which give a knowledge of the truth, that he is doing the work of God and that every talent is to be used to the glory of His name. God will be with everyone who seeks to understand the truth that he may set it before others in clear lines. God has spoken plainly and clearly. 'The Spirit and the bride say, Come. And let him that heareth say, Come.' Revelation 22:17. We are to make no delay in giving instruction to those who need it, that they may be brought to a knowledge of the truth as it is in Jesus. – *Testimonies*, vol. 6, pp. 314, 315. (1900)

Watchmen and Messengers. – The time has come when a large work should be done by the canvassers. The world is asleep, and as watchmen they are to ring the warning bell to awake the sleepers to their danger. The churches know not the time of their visitation. Often they can best learn the truth through the efforts of the canvasser. Those who go forth in the name of the Lord are His messengers to give to the multitudes who are in darkness and error the glad tidings of salvation through Christ in obeying the law of God. – *Testimonies*, vol. 6, p. 315. (1900)

Seeing Souls Converted. – Let canvassers go forth with the word of the Lord, remembering that those who obey the commandments and teach others to obey them will be rewarded by seeing souls converted, and one soul truly converted will bring others to Christ. Thus the work will advance into new territory. – *Testimonies* vol. 6, p. 315. (1900)

As Long as Probation Lasts. – As long as probation continues, there will be opportunity for the canvasser to work. When the religious denominations unite with the papacy to oppress God's people, places where there is religious freedom will be opened by evangelistic canvassing. If in one place the persecution becomes severe, let the workers do as Christ has directed. 'When they persecute you in this city, flee ye into another.' If persecution comes there, go to still another place. God will lead His people, making them a blessing in many places. Were it not for persecution they would not be so widely scattered abroad to proclaim the truth. And Christ declares: 'Ye shall not have gone over the cities of Israel, till the Son of man be come.' Matthew 10:23. Until in heaven is spoken the word, 'It is finished,' there will always be places for labor, and hearts to receive the message. – *Testimonies*, vol. 6, p. 478. (1900)

There is a great work to be done, and every effort possible must be made to reveal Christ as the sin-pardoning Saviour, Christ as the Sin Bearer, Christ as the bright and morning Star; and the Lord will give us favor before the world until our work is done. – *Testimonies*, vol. 6, pp. 20, 21. (1900)

No Higher Work. – There is no higher work than evangelistic canvassing, for it involves the performance of the highest moral duties. Those who engage in this work need always to be under the control of the Spirit of God. There must be no exalting of self. What have any of us that we did not receive from Christ? We must love as brethren, revealing our love by helping one another. We must be pitiful and courteous. We must press together, drawing in even cords. Only those who live the prayer of Christ, working it out in practical life, will stand the test that is to come upon all the world. Those who exalt self place themselves in Satan's power, preparing to receive his deceptions. The word of the Lord to His people is that we lift the standard higher and still higher. If we obey His voice, He will work with us, and our efforts will be crowned with success. In our work we shall receive rich blessings from on high and shall lay up treasure beside the throne of God.

If we only knew what is before us we would not be so dilatory in the work of the Lord.

Responsible for Work We Might Have Done. – We are in the shaking time, the time when everything that can be shaken will be shaken. The Lord will not excuse those who know the truth if they do not in word and deed obey His commands. If we make no effort to win souls to Christ we shall be held responsible for the work we might have done, but did not do because of our spiritual indolence. Those who belong to the Lord's kingdom must work earnestly for the saving of souls.

They must do their part to bind up the law and seal it among the disciples.

Who Will Go? – The Lord designs that the light which He has given on the Scriptures shall shine forth in clear, bright rays; and it is the duty of our canvassers to put forth a strong, united effort that God's design may be accomplished. A great and important work is before us. The enemy of souls realizes this, and he is using every means in his power to lead the canvasser to take up some other line of work. This order of things should be changed. God calls the canvassers back to their work. He calls for volunteers who will put all their energies and enlightenment into the work, helping wherever there is opportunity. The Master calls for everyone to do the part given him according to his ability. Who will respond to the call? Who will go forth to labor in wisdom and grace and the love of Christ for those nigh and afar off? Who will sacrifice ease and pleasure, and enter the places of error, superstition, and darkness, working earnestly and perseveringly, speaking the truth in simplicity, praying in faith, doing house-to-house labor? Who at this time will go forth without the camp, imbued with the power of the Holy Spirit, bearing reproach for Christ's sake, opening the Scriptures to the people, and calling them to repentance?

God has His workmen in every age. The call of the hour is answered by the coming of the man. Thus when the divine Voice cries, 'Whom shall I send, and who will go for Us?' the response will come, 'Here am I; send me.' Isaiah 6:8. Let all who labor effectually in the canvassing field feel in their hearts that they are doing the work of the Lord in ministering to souls who know not the truth for this time. They are sounding the note of warning in the highways and byways to prepare a people for the great day of the Lord, which is so soon to break upon the world. We have no time to lose. We must encourage this work. Who will go forth now with our publications?

The Lord imparts a fitness for the work to every man and woman who will co-operate with divine power. All the requisite talent, courage, perseverance, faith, and tact will come as they put the armor on. A great work is to be done in our world, and human agencies will surely respond to the demand. The world must hear the warning. When the call comes, 'Whom shall I send, and who will go for us?' send back the answer clear and distinct, 'Here am I; send me.' – *Testimonies*, vol. 6, pp. 331-333. (1900)

Comments of Careless Spectators. – Careless spectators may not appreciate your work or see its importance. They may think it a losing business, a life of thankless labor and self-sacrifice. But the servant of Jesus sees it in the light shining from the cross. His sacrifices appear small in comparison with those of the blessed Master, and he is glad to follow in His steps. The success of his labor affords him the purest joy and is the richest recompense for a life of patient toil. – *Testimonies*, vol. 6, p. 340. (1900)

No time to Lose. – The canvassing work is a work of great responsibility, meaning much to the men and women who engage in it. We are living in a time when there is a great work to be done, and what better opportunity can we have to give the call to the supper Christ has prepared? Those who at this time take up the canvassing work with earnestness and consecration will be greatly blessed. You have no time to lose. Give yourselves willingly and unselfishly to the doing of this work. Remember that it is evangelistic in its nature, and that it helps to give a warning which is greatly needed. – *Manuscript 113, 1901.*

CHAPTER 3

A call for colporteur evangelists

Recruits Called For. – Night after night I am standing before the people, bearing a very positive testimony, and pleading with them to be wide awake, and to take up the work of circulating our literature. – *Review and Herald*, April 20, 1905.

The canvassing field is in need of recruits. Those who engage in this work in the spirit of the Master will find entrance to the homes of those who need the truth. To these they can tell the simple story of the cross, and God will strengthen and bless them as they lead others to the light. The righteousness of Christ goes before them, and the glory of God is their rearward. – *Review and Herald*, June 16, 1903.

Arise and Shine. – The canvassing work should no longer be neglected. Many times I have been shown that there should be a more general interest in our canvassing work. The circulation of our literature is one very important means of placing before men and women the light that the Lord has committed to His church to be given to the world. The books sold by our canvassers open to many minds the unsearchable riches of Christ.

In the service of God there is work of many kinds to be

performed. In the service of the temple there were hewers of wood, as well as priests of various orders bearing various degrees of responsibility. Our church members are to arise and shine because their light has come, and the glory of the Lord has risen upon them. Let those who know the truth arouse out of sleep, and make every effort to reach the people where they are. The work of the Lord must no longer be neglected by us, and made secondary to worldly interests. We have no time to be idle or discouraged. The gospel is to be proclaimed to all the world. The publications containing the light of present truth are to go forth to all places. . . .

Why are we not more wide-awake? Each worker may now understand his special work, and receive strength to take hold of it anew. Distinct and peculiar developments of the boundless glory of God will bring tributary offerings of varied kinds to the feet of Jesus. Every new disclosure of the Saviour's love turns the balance for some soul in one direction or the other. The end of all things is at hand. The men of the world are rushing on to their ruin. Their schemes, their confederacies, are many. New devices will continually be brought in to make of no effect the counsel of God. Men are heaping up treasures of gold and silver to be consumed by the fires of the last days. – *Review and Herald*, June 2, 1903.

The Lord Calls for Many. – The new year is just before us, and plans should be laid for earnest, persevering effort in the Master's service. There is much to be done to advance the work of God. I have been instructed that the canvassing work is to be revived, and that it is to be carried forward with increasing success. It is the Lord's work, and a blessing will attend those who engage in it with earnestness and diligence. – *Review and Herald*, Jan. 20, 1903.

The Lord calls for many more to engage in the canvassing work. . . . For Christ's sake, my brethren and sisters, make the most of the hours of the new year to place the precious light of present truth before the people. The Angel of the covenant is empowering His servants to carry the truth to all parts of the world. He has sent forth His angels with the message of mercy; but, as if they did not speed on their way fast enough to satisfy His heart of yearning love, He lays on every member of His church the responsibility of proclaiming this message. 'Let him that heareth say, Come.' Every member of the church is to show his loyalty by inviting the thirsty to drink of the water of life. A chain of living witnesses is to carry the invitation to the world. Will you act your part in this great work?

Both Men and Women. – Jesus is calling for many missionaries, for men and women who will consecrate themselves to God, willing to spend and be spent in His service. Oh, can we not remember that here is a world to labor for? Shall we not move forward step by step, letting God use us as His helping hand? Shall we not place ourselves on the altar of service? Then the love of Christ will touch and transform us, make us willing for His sake to do and dare. – *Review and Herald*, Jan. 27, 1903.

Many, both men and women, can do an excellent work by canvassing for books that are full of direct, simple instruction on practical godliness. – *Manuscript 81*, 1900.

A Call to Youth. – The Lord calls upon our youth to labor as canvassers and evangelists, to do house-to-house work in places that have not yet heard the truth. He speaks to our young men, saying, 'Ye are not your own. For ye are bought with a price: therefore glorify God in your body, and in your spirit, which are God's.' Those who will go forth to the work under God's direction will be wonderfully blessed. Those who in this life do their best will obtain a fitness for the future immortal life. – *Review and Herald*, May 16, 1912.

We have a work to do. Educate, educate, educate young men to give themselves to the ministry of the word. Educate them to become canvassers, to sell those books which the Lord by His Holy Spirit has stirred minds to write. This reading matter will thus be given to a large class of people who would never hear the truth unless it was brought to their doors. This is the work of the evangelist. – *Letter 135*, 1900.

Christ calls for young men who will volunteer to carry the truth to the world. Men of spiritual stamina are wanted, men who are able to find work close at hand, because they are looking for it. The church needs new men to give energy to the ranks, men for the times, able to cope with its errors, men who will inspire with fresh zeal the flagging efforts of the few laborers, men whose hearts are warm with Christian love, and whose hands are eager to go about their Master's work. – *Manual for Canvassers*, p. 22. (1902)

Hundreds to Go. – May the Lord move upon many of our young men to enter the canvassing field as canvassing evangelists. By the canvassing work the truth is presented to thousands that otherwise would not hear it. Our time for work is short. . . .

Why is there not a more diligent seeking of the Lord, that hundreds may be filled with the Holy Spirit, and may go forth to proclaim the truth, 'the Lord working with them, and confirming the word with signs following'? Our commission is to let the light shine forth everywhere from the press. By the printed page the light reaches the isolated ones, who have no opportunity to hear the living preachers. This is a most blessed missionary work. Canvassers can be the Lord's helping hand, opening doors for the entrance of truth. . . .

We must arouse the zeal and earnestness of the canvassing agents, calling on them to take the light into the dark places of the earth. There is no release for any who have talents and capabilities. They are required to be the Lord's instruments, required to co-operate with the Lord Jesus in shedding the light of heaven into this sin-darkened world. – *Letter 21*, 1902.

Workers From Every Church. – God calls for workers from every church among us to enter His service as canvasser evangelists. God loves His church. If the members will do His will, if they will strive to impart the light to those in darkness, He will greatly bless their efforts. He represents the church as being the light of the world. Through its faithful ministrations, a multitude that no man can number will become children of God, fitted for the everlasting glory. Every part of God's dominion is to be filled with His glory. What, then, is the church doing to enlighten the world, that from all parts of the earth a

tribute of praise and prayer and thanksgiving may ascend
to Him? – *Letter 124*, 1902.

Every Believer to Help. – Let every believer scatter broadcast tracts and leaflets and books containing the message
for this time. We need colporteurs, who will go forth
to circulate our publications everywhere. – *Review and
Herald*, Nov. 12, 1903.

Men From Common Walks of Life. – In this closing work
of the gospel there is a vast field to be occupied; and, more
than ever before, the work is to enlist helpers from the
common people. Both the youth and those older in years
will be called from the field, from the vineyard, and from
the workshop, and sent forth by the Master to give His
message. Many of these have had little opportunity for education; but Christ sees in them qualifications that will enable them to fulfill His purpose. If they put their hearts
into the work, and continue to be learners, He will fit
them to labor for Him. – *Education*, pp. 269, 270. (1903)

God's Blessing Promised. – There is missionary labor to
be done in the distribution of tracts and papers, and in
canvassing for our different publications. Let none of you
think that you cannot engage in this work because it is tax-
ing, and requires time and thought. If it requires time, give
it cheerfully; and the blessing of God will rest upon you.
There never was a time when more workers were needed
than at the present. There are brethren and sisters
throughout all our ranks who should discipline themselves
to engage in this work; in all our churches something

should be done to spread the truth. It is the duty of all to study the various points of our faith, that they may be prepared to give a reason for the hope that is within them, with meekness and fear. – *Review and Herald*, April 1, 1880.

Christ Will Teach What to Say. – Many are sad and discouraged, weak in faith and trust. Let them do something to help someone more needy than themselves, and they will grow strong in God's strength. Let them engage in the good work of selling our books. Thus they will help others, and the experience gained will give them the assurance that they are God's helping hand. As they plead with the Lord to help them, He will guide them to those who are seeking for the light. Christ will be close beside them, teaching them what to say and do. By comforting others, they themselves will be comforted.

Angels Accompany and Prepare Way. – I ask you, dear Christian workers, to do what you can to circulate the books that the Lord has said should be sown broadcast throughout the world. Do your best to place them in the homes of as many people as possible. Think of how great a work can be done if a large number of believers will unite in an effort to place before the people, by the circulation of these books, the light that the Lord has said should be given them. Under divine guidance, go forward in the work, and look to the Lord for aid. The Holy Spirit will attend you. Angels of heaven will accompany you, preparing the way. – *Review and Herald*, Jan. 7, 1903.

The Consecration God Requires. – We need canvassers,

evangelists, ministers, who have received the Holy Spirit, and who are partakers of the divine nature. We need workers who are able to talk with God, and then with the people. I am alarmed as I see how many obstructions are coming in to divert men from evangelistic work, and thus hinder the work of God. . . . I warn those who should be in the canvassing work, circulating the books so much needed everywhere, to be careful not to turn from the work that the Lord has called them to. Let not the men that God has called to do gospel work become entangled with business perplexities. Let them keep their souls in the atmosphere most favorable to spirituality. . . . God wants every worker who claims to believe the present truth to consecrate himself, body, soul, and spirit, to the work of seeking to save the perishing souls around him. – *Manuscript 44*, 1903.

City Colporteurs Needed. – Books containing the precious light of present truth are lying on the shelves of our publishing houses. These should be circulated. Canvassers are needed who will enter our large cities with these books. As they go from house to house, they will find souls who are hungry for the bread of life, to whom they can speak words in season. Canvassers are needed who feel a burden for souls. You may say, 'I am not a minister. I cannot preach to the people.' No, you may not be able to preach; but you can minister, you can ask those you meet if they love the Lord Jesus. You can be an evangelist. You can be God's helping hand, working as did the disciples when Christ sent them forth. Young men, young women, you are called by the Master to take up His

work. There is a famine in the land for the pure gospel.
– *Manuscript 113*, 1901.

Workers Called to Highways and Byways. – The things of
this world are soon to perish. This is not discerned by
those who have not been divinely enlightened, who have
not kept pace with the work of God. Consecrated men
and women must go forth to sound the warning in the
highways and the byways. I urge my brethren and sisters
not to engage in work that will hinder them from proclaiming the gospel of Christ. You are God's spokesmen.
You are to speak the truth in love to perishing souls. 'Go
out into the highways and hedges, and compel them to
come in, that My house may be filled,' Christ says. Do not
these words plainly outline the work of the canvasser?
With Christ in his heart he is to go forth into the highways and byways of life, giving the invitation to the mar-
riage supper. Men of wealth and influence will come, if
they are invited. Some will refuse, but thank God, not all.

O that thousands more of our people had a realization
of the time in which we are living, and of the work to be
done in field service, in house-to-house labor. There are
many, many who know not the truth. They need to hear
the call to come to Jesus. The sorrowing are to be
cheered, the weak strengthened, the mourners comforted. The poor are to have the gospel preached to them.

The Master knows and watches over His workers, in
whatever part of His vineyard they are working. He calls
upon His church to arouse and become acquainted with
the situation. He calls upon those in our institutions to
awake and set in operation influences that will advance

His kingdom. Let them send forth laborers into the field, and then see that the interest of these laborers does not flag for lack of sympathy and of opportunities for development. – *Review and Herald*, June 2, 1903.

Scatter Books Like Leaves of Autumn. – This is a work that should be done. The end is near. Already much time has been lost, when these books should have been in circulation. Sell them far and near. Scatter them like the leaves of autumn. This work is to continue without the forbiddings of anyone. Souls are perishing out of Christ. Let them be warned of His soon appearing in the clouds of heaven. – *Review and Herald*, Aug. 13, 1908.

One Hundred Where There Is One. – The lost sheep of God's fold are scattered in every place, and the work that should be done for them is being neglected. From the light given me I know that where there is one canvasser in the field, there should be one hundred. – *Testimonies*, vol. 6. p. 315. (1900)

Assurance of Success. – A great and good work may be done by evangelistic canvassing. The Lord has given men tact and capabilities. Those who use these entrusted talents to His glory, weaving Bible principles into the web, will be given success. We are to work and pray, putting our trust in Him who will never fail. – *Testimonies*, vol. 6, p. 340. (1900)

CHAPTER 4

Selection of colporteur evangelists

Those Who Feel Burden of Service. – Since canvassing for our literature is a missionary work, it should be conducted from a missionary standpoint. Those selected as canvassers should be men and women who feel the burden of service, whose object is not to get gain, but to give light to the people. All our service is to be done to the glory of God, to give the light of truth to those who are in darkness. Selfish principles, love of gain, dignity, or position, should not be once named among us. – *Testimonies*, vol. 6, p. 317. (1900)

Care in Selecting Workers. – The canvassing work is more important than many have regarded it, and as much care and wisdom must be used in selecting the workers as in selecting men for the ministry. Young men can be trained to do much better work than has been done and on much less pay than many have received. Lift up the standard and let the self-denying and the self-sacrificing, the lovers of God and of humanity, join the army of workers. Let them come, not expecting ease, but to be brave and of good courage under rebuffs and hardships. Let those come who can give a good report of our publications because they themselves appreciate their value. – *Testimonies*, vol. 5, pp. 405, 406. (1885)

Our brethren should show discretion in selecting canvassers and colporteurs, unless they have made up their minds to have the truth misapprehended and misrepresented. They should give all real workers good wages; but the sum should not be increased to buy canvassers, for this course hurts them. It makes them selfish and spendthrifts. Seek to impress them with the spirit of true missionary work and with the qualifications necessary to ensure success. The love of Jesus in the soul will lead the canvasser to feel it a privilege to labor to diffuse light. He will study, plan, and pray over the matter. – *Testimonies*, vol. 5, p. 403. (1885)

Some Better Adapted Than Others. – Some are better adapted than others for doing a certain work; therefore it is not correct to think that everyone can be a canvasser. Some have no special adaptability for this work; but they are not, because of this, to be regarded as faithless or unwilling. The Lord is not unreasonable in His requirements. The church is as a garden in which is a variety of flowers, each with its own peculiarities. Though in many respects all may differ, yet each has a value of its own.

God does not expect that with their different temperaments His people will each be prepared for any and every place. Let all remember that there are varied trusts. It is not the work of any man to prescribe the work of any other man contrary to his own convictions of duty. It is right to give counsel and suggest plans; but every man should be left free to seek direction from God, whose he is and whom he serves. – *Testimonies*, vol. 6, pp. 333. 334. (1900)

Young men and young women who should be engaged in the ministry, in Bible work, and in the canvassing work should not be bound down to mechanical employment. – Review and Herald, May 16, 1912.

Men of Good Address, Tact, and Foresight. – Missionaries are wanted everywhere. In all parts of the field canvassers should be selected, not from the floating element in society, not from among men and women who are good for nothing else and have made a success of nothing, but from among those who have good address, tact, keen foresight, and ability. Such are needed to make a success as colporteurs, canvassers, and agents. Men suited to this work undertake it, but some injudicious minister will flatter them that their gift should be employed in the desk instead of simply in the work of the colporteur. Thus this work is belittled. They are influenced to get a license to preach; and the very ones who might have been trained to make good missionaries to visit families at their homes and talk and pray with them are caught up to make poor ministers; and the field where so much labor is needed, and where so much good might be accomplished for the cause, is neglected. The efficient colporteur, as well as the minister, should have a sufficient remuneration for his services if his work is faithfully done. – Testimonies, vol. 4, pp. 389, 390. (1880)

Those of the Best Talent. – Everyone is not fitted for this work. Those of the best talent and ability, who will take hold of the work understandingly and systematically, and carry it forward with persevering energy, are the ones who should be selected. There should be a most thoroughly organized plan; and this should be faithfully carried out. Churches in every place should feel the deepest interest in the tract and missionary work. – *Testimonies*, vol. 4, p. 390. (1880)

Religious Experience Needed. – Let Christian youth be selected to circulate the books containing present truth. Youth who have no religious experience should not be accepted as canvassers for our books, because they cannot properly represent the precious truth to be presented. To send such youth into the canvassing field is unjust to them and to the Lord's work. This is a sacred work, and those who enter it should be able to bear witness for Christ. – *Review and Herald*, Oct. 7, 1902.

Canvassing is the best way in which to obtain experience. Be sure that these souls are soundly converted before encouraging them to labor in any line. Then let them work, and God will work with them. – *Manuscript 126, 1899*.

A Sacred Work. – The canvassing work should be considered as sacred, and those who have unclean hands and defiled hearts should not be encouraged to enter upon it. The angels of God cannot accompany the unconsecrated to the homes of the people; therefore all those who are not converted, whose thoughts are corrupt, who will leave the taint of their imperfections upon everything they touch, should refrain from handling the truth of God. – *Review and Herald*, May 20, 1890.

CHAPTER 5

Our students and colporteur evangelism

A Divine Plan for Our Students. – The Lord has instituted a plan whereby many of the students in our schools can learn practical lessons needful to success in afterlife. He has given us the privilege of handling precious books that have been dedicated to the advancement of our educational and sanitarium work. In the very handling of these books, the youth will meet with many experiences that will teach them how to cope with problems that await them in the regions beyond. During their school life, as they handle these books, many learn how to approach people courteously, and how to exercise tact in conversing with them on different points of present truth. As they meet with a degree of success financially, some will learn lessons of thrift and economy, which will be of great advantage to them when they are sent out as missionaries. – *Review and Herald*, June 4, 1908.

Schools to Prepare Colporteur Evangelists. – Our schools have been established by the Lord; and if they are conducted in harmony with His purpose, the youth sent to them will quickly be prepared to engage in various branches of missionary work. Some will be trained to enter the field as missionary nurses, some as canvassers, some as evangelists, some as teachers, and some as gospel ministers. – *Review and Herald*, Oct. 15, 1903.

Opportunity for Student Colporteurs. – When school closes, there will be opportunity for many to go out into the field as evangelistic canvassers. The faithful colporteur finds his way into many homes, where he leaves precious reading matter containing the truth for this time. – *Review and Herald*, Aug. 27, 1903.

Learn in the School of Christ. – As students, you are ever to be learning in the school of Christ; you are to bring your entrusted capital of physical and mental energy into your work. God will not accept of a divided heart. There are men and women who should be educating themselves for canvassers, and for Bible readers [Bible instructors]. They should put away every unholy thought and corrupting practice, that they may be sanctified through the truth. They should be partakers of the divine nature, having escaped the corruption that is in the world through lust. Nothing less than the power of God will make and keep you right. You are to offer to God nothing less than your best. You should do better and better work as you put in practice what you learn. – *Review and Herald*, May 20, 1890.

A Means of Education. – I have had special light in regard to the canvassing work, and the impression and burden does not leave me. This work is a means of education. It is an excellent school for those who are qualifying themselves to enter the ministry. Those who take up this work as they should place themselves where they learn of Christ and follow His example. Angels are commissioned to go forth with those who take up this work in true humility. – *Manuscript 26*, 1901.

The very best education young men can obtain is by entering the canvassing field and working from house to house. In this work they will find opportunity to speak the words of life. Thus they will sow the seeds of truth. Let young men show that they have resting on them a burden from the Lord. The only way for them to prove that they can stand firm in God, having on the whole armor, is by doing faithfully the work God has given them to do. – *Manuscript 75*, 1900.

True 'Higher Education.' – We must not discourage our brethren, weakening their hands so that the work which God desires to accomplish through them shall not be done. Let not too much time be occupied in fitting up men to do missionary work. Instruction is necessary, but let all remember that Christ is the Great Teacher and the Source of all true wisdom. Let young and old consecrate themselves to God, take up the work, and go forward, laboring in humility under the control of the Holy Spirit. Let those who have been in school go out into the field and put to a practical use the knowledge they have gained. If canvassers will do this, using the ability which God has given them, seeking counsel from Him, and combining the work of selling books with personal labor for the people, their talents will increase by exercise, and they will learn many practical lessons which they could not possibly learn in school. The education obtained in this practical way may properly be termed higher education. – *Testimonies*, vol. 6, pp. 330, 331. (1900)

An Invaluable Experience. – All who desire an opportunity for true ministry, and who will give themselves unreservedly to God, will find in the canvassing work opportunities to speak upon many things pertaining to the future, immortal life. The experience thus gained will be of the greatest value to those who are fitting themselves for the ministry. It is the accompaniment of the Holy Spirit of God that prepares workers, both men and women, to become pastors to the flock of God. As they cherish the thought that Christ is their Companion, a holy awe, a sacred joy, will be felt by them amid all their trying experiences and all their tests. They will learn how to pray as they work. They will be educated in patience, kindness, affability, and helpfulness. They will practice true Christian courtesy, bearing in mind that Christ, their Companion, cannot approve of harsh, unkind words or feelings. Their words will be purified. The power of speech will be regarded as a precious talent, lent them to do a high and holy work. The human agent will learn how to represent the divine Companion with whom he is associated. To that unseen Holy One he will show respect and reverence because he is wearing His yoke and is learning His pure, holy ways. Those who have faith in this divine Attendant will develop. They will be gifted with power to clothe the message of truth with a sacred beauty. – *Testimonies*, vol. 6, p. 322. (1900)

A Preparation for the Ministry. – Some men whom God was calling to the work of the ministry have entered the field as canvassers. I have been instructed that this is an excellent preparation if their object is to disseminate light, to bring the truths of God's word directly to the home circle. In conversation the way will often be opened for them to speak of the religion of the Bible. If the work is entered upon as it should be, families will be visited, the workers will manifest Christian tenderness and love for souls, and great good will be the result. This will be an excellent experience for any who have the ministry in view.

Those who are fitting for the ministry can engage in no other occupation that will give them so large an experience as will the canvassing work. – *Testimonies*, vol. 6, p. 334. (1900)

There are more difficulties in this work than in some other branches of business; but the lessons learned, the tact and discipline acquired, will fit you for other fields of usefulness, where you can minister to souls. Those who poorly learn their lesson, and are careless and abrupt in approaching persons, would show the same want of tact and skill in dealing with minds, should they enter the ministry. . . .

In evangelistic canvassing, young men may become better prepared for ministerial labor than by spending many years in school. – *Manual for Canvassers*, pp. 41, 42. (1902)

The Essential Knowledge. – To those who are attending school that they may learn how to do the work of God more perfectly, I would say: Remember that it is only by a daily consecration to God that you can become soul winners. There have been those who were unable to go to school because they were too poor to pay their way. But when they became sons and daughters of God they took hold of their work where they were, laboring for those around them. Though destitute of the knowledge obtained in school, they consecrated themselves to God, and God worked through them. Like the disciples when called from their nets to follow Christ, they learned precious lessons from the Saviour. They linked themselves with the Great Teacher, and knowledge they gained from the Scriptures qualified them to speak to others of Christ. Thus they became truly wise, because they were not too wise in their own estimation to receive instruction from above. The renewing power of the Holy Spirit gave them practical, saving energy.

The knowledge of the most learned man, if he has not learned in Christ's school, is foolishness so far as leading souls to Christ is concerned. God can work with those only who will accept the invitation: 'Come unto Me, all ye that labor and are heavy-laden, and I will give you rest. Take My yoke upon you, and learn of Me; for I am meek and lowly in heart: and ye shall find rest unto your souls. For My yoke is easy, and My burden is light.' Matthew 11:28-30. – *Testimonies*, vol. 6, p. 318. (1900)

CHAPTER 6

A soul-winning work

A Means of Bringing Souls to Christ. – We need to realize the importance of the canvassing work as one great means of finding out those who are in peril and bringing them to Christ. Canvassers should never be prohibited from speaking of the love of Christ, from telling their experience in their service for the Master. They should be free to speak or to pray with those who are awakened. The simple story of Christ's love for man will open doors for them, even to the homes of unbelievers. – *Testimonies*, vol. 6, p. 324. (1900)

He who takes up the work of canvassing as he should must be both an educator and a student. While he tries to teach others he himself must learn to do the work of an evangelist. As canvassers go forth into the field with humble hearts, full of earnest activity, they will find many opportunities to speak a word in season to souls ready to die in discouragement. After laboring for these needy ones they will be able to say: 'Ye were sometimes darkness, but now are ye light in the Lord.' Ephesians 5:8. As they see the sinful course of others they can say: 'Such were some of you: but ye are washed, but ye are sanctified, but ye are justified in the name of the Lord Jesus, and by the Spirit of our God.' 1 Corinthians 6:11. – *Testimonies*, vol. 6, p. 335. (1900)

My brethren and sisters, remember that one day you will stand before the Lord of all the earth, to give an account of the deeds done in the body. Then your work will appear as it really is. The vineyard is large, and the Lord is calling for laborers. Do not allow anything to keep you from the work of soul saving. The canvassing work is a most successful way of saving souls. Will you not try it? – *Review and Herald*, June 2, 1903.

Colporteur to Reveal Christ. – Christ's interests are the first and the highest of all interests. He has a property in this world that He wishes secured, saved for His everlasting kingdom. It is for His Father's glory and for His own glory that His messengers shall go forth in His name; for they and He are one. They are to reveal Him to the world. His interests are their interests. If they will be colaborers with Him, they will be made heirs of God and joint heirs with Christ to an immortal inheritance. – *Review and Herald*, June 2, 1903.

Speak Words of Truth. – The canvassing work is a work of great responsibility, and it means much not only to those who are engaged in it, but to the people for whom they labor. Let the canvasser remember that his work is evangelistic in its nature, and that God wants those whom he meets to be saved. Let him keep his heart under the influence of the Holy Spirit. Let him keep the Bible near him for reference, and when an opportunity presents itself to speak words of truth, let him pray for grace to speak wisely, that to those to whom he speaks his words may be a savor of life unto life. – *Review and Herald*, June 16, 1903.

To Hunt and Fish for Souls. – Canvasser evangelists are needed, to hunt and fish for souls. The canvassing work should now be earnestly and decidedly taken up. The canvasser whose heart is meek and lowly can accomplish much good. Going out two and two, canvassers can reach a class that cannot be reached by our camp meetings. From family to family they carry the message of truth. Thus they come into close touch with the people, and find many opportunities to speak of the Saviour. Let them sing and pray with those who become interested in the truths they have to give. Let them speak to families the words of Christ. They may expect success; for theirs is the promise, 'Lo, I am with you alway, even unto the end of the world.' Canvassers who go forth in the spirit of the Master have the companionship of heavenly beings.

I beg those bearing responsibilities in God's cause to let no commercial enterprises interpose between them and the work of soul saving. Let no business be allowed to absorb the time and talents of workers who ought to be engaged in preparing a people for the coming of the Lord. The truth is to go forth as a lamp that burneth. Time is short; the enemy will make every effort to magnify in our minds matters of lesser consequence, and to lead us to regard lightly the very work that most needs to be done. – *Review and Herald*, June 2, 1903.

Reach All Classes. – In order to reach all classes, we must meet them where they are. They will seldom seek us of their own accord. Not alone from the pulpit are the hearts of men touched by divine truth. There is another field of labor, humbler, it may be, but fully as promising. It is found in the home of the lowly, and in the mansion of the great. – *The Desire of Ages*, p. 152. (1898)

Those in the Highways. – Take the books to businessmen, to teachers of the gospel, whose minds have not been called to the special truths for this time. The message is to be given 'in the highways,' – to men who take an active part in the world's work, to the teachers and leaders of the people. Thousands can be reached in the most simple, humble way. The most intellectual, those who are looked upon as the world's most gifted men and women, are often refreshed by the simple words of one who loves God, and who can speak of that love as naturally as the worldling speaks of the things that interest him most deeply. Often the words well prepared and studied have but little influence. But the true, honest expression of a son or daughter of God, spoken in natural simplicity, has power to open the door to hearts that have long been closed against Christ and His love. – *Review and Herald*, Jan. 20, 1903.

Books will reach those who can be reached in no other way, – those living far from any large settlement. I call these the byway hearers. To such ones our canvassers are to carry the books containing the message of salvation.

Our canvassers are to be God's evangelists, going from house to house in out-of-the-way places, and opening the Scriptures to those they meet. They will find those who are willing and anxious to learn from the Scriptures. . . .

I greatly desire to do all in my power to reach those in

the highways and the byways. – *Letter 155*, 1903.

In the Thoroughfares of Travel. – In the world-renowned health resorts and centers of tourist traffic, crowded with many thousands of seekers after health and pleasure, there should be stationed ministers and canvassers capable of arresting the attention of the multitudes. Let these workers watch their chance to present the message for this time, and hold meetings as they have opportunity. Let them be quick to seize opportunities to speak to the people. Accompanied by the power of the Holy Spirit, let them meet the people with the message borne by John the Baptist: 'Repent ye: for the kingdom of heaven is at hand.' The word of God is to be presented with clearness and power, that those who have ears to hear, may hear the truth. Thus the gospel of present truth will be placed in the way of those who know it not, and will be accepted by not a few, and carried by them to their own homes in all parts of the earth. – *Review and Herald*, Jan. 25, 1906.

Help the Intemperate. – In your work you will meet with those who are fighting against appetite. Speak words that will strengthen and encourage them. Do not let Satan quench the last spark of hope in their hearts. Of the erring, trembling one, struggling with evil, Christ says, 'Let him come unto Me;' and He places His hands underneath him, and lifts him up. The work that Christ did, you, as His evangelists, can do as you go from place to place. Labor in faith, expecting that souls will be won to Him who gave His life that men and women might stand on God's side. Draw with God to win the drunkard and the tobacco devotee from the habits which debase them till they are below the level of the beasts that perish. – *Review and Herald*, Jan. 7, 1903.

Pray for Sick and Discouraged. – Christ was sowing the seeds of truth wherever He was, and as His followers you can witness for the Master, doing a most precious work in fireside labor. In thus coming close to the people you will often find those who are sick and discouraged. If you are pressing close to the side of Christ, wearing His yoke, you will daily learn of Him how to carry messages of peace and comfort to the sorrowing and disappointed, the sad and brokenhearted. You can point the discouraged ones to the word of God and take the sick to the Lord in prayer. As you pray, speak to Christ as you would to a trusted, much-loved friend. Maintain a sweet, free, pleasant dignity, as a child of God. This will be recognized. – *Testimonies*, vol. 6, pp. 323, 324. (1900)

With a Prayer on the Lips. – The claims of God are to be ever before us. We should never forget that we are to give an account for the deeds done in the body. Weighted with this thought, canvassers will watch for souls, and their prayer will go forth from unfeigned lips for wisdom to speak a word in season to those in need of help. Such workers will continually be elevating and purifying the soul through obedience to the truth. They will have a true sense of the value of the soul, and will make the most of every opportunity to make known the riches of the grace of Christ. Let the canvasser go forth with the prayer upon his lips, 'Lord, what wilt Thou have me to do?' Let him labor as in the sight of God, and in the presence of heavenly angels; let him desire in all things to be approved by God; and his work will not be fruitless.

We need far less controversy, and far more presentation of Christ. Our Redeemer is the center of all our faith and hope. Those who can present His matchless love, and inspire hearts to give Him their best and holiest affections, are doing work that is great and holy. By diligence in canvassing, by faithfully presenting to the people the cross of Calvary, the canvasser doubles his usefulness. But while we present these methods of work, we cannot lay out an undeviating line for everyone to follow. Circumstances alter cases. . . .

Speak of Christ's Love. – Often doctrinal subjects are presented with no special effect; for men expect others to press upon them their doctrines; but when the matchless love of Christ is dwelt upon, His grace impresses the heart. There are many who are sincerely seeking for light, who know not what they must do to be saved. Oh, tell them of the love of God, of the sacrifice made on Calvary's cross to save the perishing! Tell them to place their will on the side of God's will; and 'if any man will do His will, he shall know of the doctrine, whether it be of God.' John 7:17. – *Manual for Canvassers*, pp. 36-38. (1902)

Avoid Controverted Points. – Some who labor in the canvassing field have a zeal that is not according to knowledge. Because of their lack of wisdom, because they have been so much inclined to act the minister and theologian, it has been almost a necessity to place restrictions upon our canvassers. When the Lord's voice calls, 'Whom shall I send, and who will go for Us?' the Divine Spirit puts it into hearts to respond: 'Here am I; send me.' Isaiah 6:8. But bear in mind that the live coal from the altar must first touch your lips. Then the words you speak will be wise and holy words. Then you will have wisdom to know what to say and what to leave unsaid. You will not try to reveal your smartness as theologians. You will be careful not to arouse a combative spirit or excite prejudice by introducing controverted points of doctrine. You will find enough to talk about that will not excite opposition, but that will open the heart to desire a deeper knowledge of God's word.

Ready to Give Answer. – The Lord desires you to be soul winners; therefore, while you should not force doctrinal points upon the people, you should 'be ready always to give an answer to every man that asketh you a reason of the hope that is in you with meekness and fear.' 1 Peter 3:15. Why fear? Fear lest your words should savor of self-importance, lest unadvised words be spoken, lest the words and manner should not be after Christ's likeness. Connect firmly with Christ, and present the truth as it is in Him. – *Testimonies*, vol. 6, pp. 324, 325. (1900)

Lift Up Christ. – Work as Paul worked. Wherever he was, whether before scowling Pharisee or Roman authority, rich or poor, learned or ignorant, the cripple at Lystra or the convicted sinners in the Macedonian dungeon, he lifted up Christ as the One who hates sin and

loves the sinner, the One who bore our sins that
He might impart to us His righteousness. – *Manual for
Canvassers*, p. 34. (1902)

The Minister as Canvasser. – The intelligent, God-fearing, truth-loving canvasser should be respected; for he
occupies a position equal to that of the gospel minister.
Many of our young ministers and those who are fitting
for the ministry would, if truly converted, do much good
by working in the canvassing field. And by meeting the
people and presenting to them our publications they
would gain an experience which they cannot gain by simply preaching. As they went from house to house they
could converse with the people, carrying with them the
fragrance of Christ's life. In thus endeavoring to bless
others they would themselves be blessed; they would
obtain an experience in faith; their knowledge of the
Scriptures would greatly increase; and they would be
constantly learning how to win souls for Christ.

All our ministers should feel free to carry with them
books to dispose of wherever they go. Wherever a minister goes, he can leave a book in the family where he
stays, either selling it or giving it to them. Much of this
work was done in the early history of the message. Ministers acted as colporteurs, using the means obtained
from the sale of the books to help in the advancement of
the work in places where help was needed. These can
speak intelligently in regard to this method of work; for
they have had an experience in this line.

Let none think that it belittles a minister of the gospel
to engage in canvassing as a means of carrying truth to

the people. In doing this work he is laboring in the same manner as did the apostle Paul, who says: 'Ye know, from the first day that I came into Asia, after what manner I have been with you at all seasons, serving the Lord with all humility of mind, and with many tears, and temptations, which befell me by the lying in wait of the Jews: and how I kept back nothing that was profitable unto you, but have showed you, and have taught you publicly, and from house to house, testifying both to the Jews, and also to the Greeks, repentance toward God, and faith toward our Lord Jesus Christ.' Acts 20:18-21. The eloquent Paul, to whom God manifested Himself in a wonderful manner, went from house to house in all humility of mind, and with many tears and temptations. – *Testimonies*, vol. 6, pp. 321-322. (1900)

As Important as Preaching. – The ministerial evangelist who engages in the canvassing work is performing a service fully as important as that of preaching the gospel before a congregation Sabbath after Sabbath. God looks upon the faithful evangelistic canvasser with as much approval as He looks upon any faithful minister. Both workers have light, and both are to shine in their respective spheres of influence. God calls upon every man to co-operate with the great Medical Missionary Worker, and to go forth into the highways and byways. Each man, in his particular line of service, has a work to do for God. Such laborers, if converted, are true missionaries. – *Letter 186*, 1903.

There are some who are adapted to the work of the colporteur and who can accomplish more in this line than by preaching. If the Spirit of Christ dwells in their hearts, they will find opportunity to present His word to others and to direct minds to the special truths for this time. – *Testimonies*, vol. 6, p. 323. (1900)

Joy in Service. – It was Christ's joy to help those in need of help, to seek the lost, to rescue the perishing, to lift up the bowed down, to heal the sick, to speak words of sympathy and consolation to the sorrowing and the distressed. The more fully we are imbued with His Spirit, the more earnestly we shall work for those around us; and the more we do for others, the greater will be our love for the work, and the greater our delight in following the Master. Our hearts will be filled with the love of God; and with earnestness and convincing power we shall speak of the crucified Saviour.

I ask those to whom the light of truth has come: What are you going to do during the year that is just opening? Will you stop to quarrel with one another, to weaken and destroy the faith of humanity in humanity? or will you devote your time to strengthening the things that remain, that are ready to die? As our people engage in earnest work for the Master, complaints will cease to be heard. Many will be roused from the despondency that is ruining them body and soul. As they work for others, they will have much that is helpful to speak of when they assemble to worship God. The testimonies they bear will not be dark and gloomy, but full of joy and courage. Instead of thinking and talking about the faults of their brethren and sisters, and about their own trials, they will think and talk of the love of Christ, and will strive

earnestly to become more efficient workers for Him. –
Review and Herald, Jan. 7, 1903.

Section II

The qualified colporteur

CHAPTER 7

Wholly surrendered to God

The First Essential. – Those who engage in the canvassing work should first give themselves wholly and unreservedly to God. Christ has invited them, 'Come unto Me, all ye that labor and are heavy-laden, and I will give you rest. Take My yoke upon you, and learn of Me; for I am meek and lowly in heart: and ye shall find rest unto your souls. For My yoke is easy, and My burden is light.' – *Manuscript 26,* 1901.

Redeem the Time. – If you have neglected the sowing time, if you have allowed God-given opportunities to pass unimproved, if you have given yourselves up to self-pleasing, will you not now repent, before it is forever too late, and strive to redeem the time? The obligation to use your talents in the Master's service rests heavily upon you. Come to the Lord, and make an entire surrender of all to Him. You cannot afford to lose one day. Take up your neglected work. Put away your querulous unbelief, your envy and evil thinking, and go to work, in humble faith, and with earnest prayer to the Lord to pardon you for your years of unconsecration. Ask the Lord for help. If you seek Him earnestly, with the whole heart, you will find Him, and He will strengthen and bless you. – *Review and Herald,* Jan. 7, 1903.

Be Humble and Teachable. – In choosing men and women for His service, God does not ask whether they possess learning or eloquence or worldly wealth. He asks: 'Do they walk in such humility that I can teach them My way? Can I put My words into their lips? Will they represent Me?'

God can use every person just in proportion as He can put His Spirit into the soul temple. The work that He will accept is the work that reflects His image. His followers are to bear, as their credentials to the world, the ineffaceable characteristics of His immortal principles. – *Testimonies*, vol. 7, p. 144. (1902)

Why Many Have Failed. – Canvassers need to be daily converted to God, that their words and deeds may be a savor of life unto life, that they may exert a saving influence. The reason why many have failed in the canvassing work is that they were not genuine Christians; they did not know the spirit of conversion. They had a theory as to how the work should be done, but they did not feel their dependence upon God.

Changed by Beholding. – Canvassers, remember that in the books you handle you are presenting, not the cup containing the wine of Babylon, doctrines of error dealt to the kings of the earth, but the cup full of the preciousness of the truths of redemption. Will you yourselves drink of it? Your minds can be brought into captivity to the will of Christ, and He can put upon you His own superscription. By beholding, you will become changed from glory to glory, from character to character. God wants you to come to the front, speaking the words He will give you. He wants you to show that you place a high estimate upon humanity, humanity that has been purchased by the precious blood of the Saviour. When you fall upon the Rock and are broken, you will experience the power of Christ, and others will recognize the power of the truth upon your hearts. – *Testimonies*, vol. 6, pp. 317, 318. (1900)

Put on Christ. – No one can be a successful soul winner till he himself has settled the question of surrender to God. We are individually to put on the Lord Jesus Christ. To each one of us He must become wisdom, righteousness, sanctification, and redemption. When our faith lays hold upon Christ as our personal Saviour, we shall place Him before others in a new light. And when the people behold Christ as He is, they will not wrangle over doctrines; they will flee to Him for pardon, purity, and eternal life.

The difficulty most to be dreaded is that the canvasser who meets these inquiring souls has not himself been converted; that he does not himself know by experience the love of Christ which passes knowledge. If he himself has not this knowledge, how can he tell others the precious old, old story? The people need to be taught the very essence of true faith, the way to accept Christ and to confide in Him as their personal Saviour. They need to know how they may follow His steps whithersoever He goes. Let the feet of the worker follow step by step the footprints of Jesus, and mark out no other way in which to proceed heavenward. . . .

Draw Men to the Redeemer. – Many professed Christians have broken away from Christ, the great center, and they make themselves a center; but if they would be successful in attracting others to the Saviour, they must themselves flee back to Him, and realize their utter dependence upon His grace. Satan has tried to the uttermost to sever the chain that unites men to God; he desires to bind their souls to his own car, and make them slaves in his service; but we are to work against him, and drawn men to the Redeemer. – *Manual for Canvassers*, pp. 38, 39. (1902)

Soul Brought to Jesus in Safekeeping. – When a soul has been brought to Christ through this personal labor, leave the surrendered, humbled heart for God to work with; let God urge upon him just such service as He sees fit. God has promised that His grace shall be sufficient for everyone who will come unto Him. Those who surrender to Jesus, who open the door of the heart and invite Him in, will be in safekeeping. He says, 'I am the way, the truth, and the life.' John 14:6. Possessing Jesus, they will possess truth. They will be complete in Him. – *Manual for Canvassers*, pp. 38, 39. (1902)

Absolute Honesty. – If the canvasser pursues a wrong course, if he utters falsehood or practices deception, he loses his own self-respect. He may not be conscious that God sees him and is acquainted with every business transaction, that holy angels are weighing his motives and listening to his words, and that his reward will be according to his works; but if it were possible to conceal his wrongdoing from human and divine inspection, the fact that he himself knows it, is degrading to his mind and character. One act does not determine the character, but it breaks down the barrier, and the next temptation is more readily entertained, until finally a habit of prevarication and dishonesty in business is formed, and the man cannot be trusted.

There are too many in families and in the church who make little account of glaring inconsistencies. There are young men who appear what they are not. They seem honest and true; but they are like whited sepulchers, fair without, but corrupt to the core. The heart is spotted, stained with sin; and thus the record stands in the heavenly courts. A process has been going on in the mind that has made them callous, past feeling. But if their characters, weighed in the balances of the sanctuary, are pronounced wanting in the great day of God, it will be a calamity that they do not now comprehend. Truth, precious, untarnished truth, is to be a part of the character.

Purity of Life. – Whatever way is chosen, the path of life is beset with perils. If the workers in any branch of the cause become careless and inattentive to their eternal interests, they are meeting with great loss. The tempter will find access to them. He will spread nets for their feet, and will lead them in uncertain paths. Those only are safe whose hearts are garrisoned with pure principles. Like David they will pray: 'Hold up my goings in Thy paths, that my footsteps slip not.' A constant battle must be kept up with the selfishness and corruption of the human heart. Often the wicked seem to be prospered in their way; but those who forget God, even for an hour or a moment, are in a dangerous path. They may not realize its perils; but ere they are aware, habit, like an iron band, holds them in subjection to the evil with which they have tampered. God despises their course, and His blessing will not attend them.

No Tampering With Sin. – I have seen that young men undertake this work without connecting themselves with heaven. They place themselves in the way of temptation to show their bravery. They laugh at the folly of others. They know the right way; they know how to conduct themselves. How easily they can resist temptation! How vain to think of their falling! But they make not God their defense. Satan has an insidious snare prepared for them, and they themselves become the sport of fools.

Our great adversary has agents that are constantly hunting for an opportunity to destroy souls, as a lion hunts his prey. Shun them, young man; for, while they appear to be your friends, they will slyly introduce evil ways and practices. They flatter you with their lips, and offer to help and guide you; but their steps take hold on hell. If you listen to their counsel, it may be the turning point in your life. One safeguard removed from conscience, the indulgence of one evil habit, a single neglect of the high claims of duty, may be the beginning of a course of deception that will pass you into the ranks of those who are serving Satan, while you are all the time professing to love God and His cause. A moment of thoughtlessness, a single misstep, may turn the whole current of your lives in the wrong direction. And you may never know what caused your ruin until the sentence is pronounced: 'Depart from Me, ye that work iniquity.'

Avoid Evil Associates. – Some young men know that what I have said fairly describes their course. Their ways are not hidden from the Lord, although they may be hidden from their best friends, even their fathers and mothers. I have little hope that some of these will ever change their course of hypocrisy and deception. Others who have erred are seeking to redeem themselves. May the dear Jesus help them to set their faces as a flint against all falsehoods and the flatteries of those who would weaken their purpose to do right or who would insinuate doubts or infidel sentiments to shake their faith in the truth. Young friends, do not spend an hour in the company of those who would unfit you for the pure and sacred work of God. Do nothing before strangers that you would not do before your father and mother, or that you would be ashamed of before Christ and the holy angels.

Some may think these cautions are not needed by Sabbathkeepers, but those to whom they apply know what I mean. I tell you, young men, to beware; for you can do nothing that is not open to the eyes of angels and of God. You cannot do an evil work and others not be affected by it. While your course of action reveals what kind of material is used in your own character building, it also has a powerful influence over others. Never lose sight of the fact that you belong to God, that He has bought you with a price, and you must render an account to Him for all His entrusted talents. No one should have any part in the work of the canvasser or colporteur whose hand is defiled with sin or whose heart is not right with God, for such persons will surely dishonor the cause of truth. Those who are workers in the missionary field need God to guide them. They should be careful to start right and then keep quietly and firmly on in the path of rectitude. They should be decided, for Satan is determined and persevering in his efforts to overthrow them.

– *Testimonies*, vol. 5, pp. 396-399. (1885)

Constant Dependence on God. – He who in his work meets with trials and temptations should profit by these experiences, learning to lean more decidedly upon God. He should feel his dependence every moment.

No complaint should be cherished in his heart or be uttered by his lips. When successful, he should take no glory to himself, for his success is due to the working of God's angels upon the heart. And let him remember that both in the time of encouragement and the time of discouragement the heavenly messengers are always beside him. He should acknowledge the goodness of the Lord, praising Him with cheerfulness.

Christ laid aside His glory and came to this earth to suffer for sinners. If we meet with hardships in our work, let us look to Him who is the Author and Finisher of our faith. Then we shall not fail nor be discouraged. We shall endure hardness as good soldiers of Jesus Christ. Remember what He says of all true believers: 'We are laborers together with God: ye are God's husbandry, ye are God's building.' 1 Corinthians 3:9. – *Testimonies*, vol. 6, pp. 334, 335. (1900)

The World's Greatest Need. – The greatest want of the world is the want of men, – men who will not be bought or sold; men who in their inmost souls are true and honest; men who do not fear to call sin by its right name; men whose conscience is as true to duty as the needle to the pole; men who will stand for the right though the heavens fall. – *Education*, p. 57. (1903)

CHAPTER 8

Fully prepared

Thorough Preparation. – Very much more efficient work can be done in the canvassing field than has yet been done. The canvasser should not rest satisfied unless he is constantly improving. He should make thorough preparation, but should not be content with a set form of words; he should give the Lord a chance to work with his efforts and impress his mind. The love of Jesus abiding in his heart will enable him to devise means to gain access to individuals and families. – *Testimonies*, vol. 5, p. 396. (1885)

Let a class of canvassers be fitted up, by thorough instruction and drill, to handle the publications that shall come forth from the press. – *Letter 66*, 1901.

Knowledge of God's Word. – The minds of all should be stored with a knowledge of the truths of God's word, that they may be prepared, at any moment when required, to present from the storehouse things new and old. – *Testimonies*, vol. 4, p. 415. (1880)

A Knowledge of the Book You Sell. – Canvassers should thoroughly acquaint themselves with the book they are handling and be able readily to call attention to the important chapters. – *Testimonies*, vol. 6, p. 338. (1900)

Intellectual and Heart Culture. – Young men are wanted who are men in understanding, who appreciate the intellectual faculties that God has given them, and who cultivate them with the utmost care. Exercise enlarges these faculties, and if heart culture is not neglected, the character will be well balanced. The means of improvement are within the reach of all. Then let none disappoint the Master, when He comes seeking for fruit, by presenting nothing but leaves. A resolute purpose, sanctified by the grace of Christ, will do wonders. – *Testimonies*, vol. 5, p. 403. (1885)

Let canvassers be faithful students, learning how to make their work successful; and while thus employed, let them keep their eyes and ears and understanding open to receive wisdom from God, that they may know how to help those who are perishing for lack of a knowledge of Christ. Let every worker concentrate his energies and use his powers for the highest of all service, to recover men from the snare of Satan and bind them to God, making the chain of dependence through Jesus Christ fast to the throne encircled with the rainbow of promise. – *Testimonies*, vol. 6, pp. 339, 340. (1900)

Responsibility of Teachers of Canvassers. – Teachers in the canvassing work have grave responsibilities to bear. Those who rightly comprehend their position, will direct and instruct those under their care with a sense of their personal accountability, and will inspire others to fidelity in the cause. They will be much in prayer, they will understand that their words and actions are making impressions that will not be easily effaced, but will be as enduring as eternity. They will realize that no other can come after them and correct their mistakes, or supply their deficiencies. How important it is, then, that the teachers' subject, manner, and spirit are after God's order. – *Review and Herald*, May 20, 1890.

To Be Educated and Trained. – The presidents of our conferences and others in responsible positions have a duty to do in this matter, that the different branches of our work may receive equal attention. Canvassers are to be educated and trained to do the work required in selling the books upon present truth which the people need. There is need of men of deep Christian experience, men of well-balanced minds, strong, well-educated men, to engage in this work. The Lord desires those to take hold of the canvassing work who are capable of educating others, who can awaken in promising young men and women an interest in this line, leading them to take up the book work and handle it successfully. Some have the talent, education, and experience which would enable them to educate the youth for the canvassing work in such a way that much more would be accomplished than is now being done.

Experienced With Inexperienced. – Those who have gained an experience in this work have a special duty to perform in teaching others. Educate, educate, educate young men and women to sell the books which the Lord by His Holy Spirit has stirred His servants to write. God desires us to be faithful in educating those who accept the truth, that they may believe to a purpose and work intelligently in the Lord's way. Let inexperienced persons be connected with experienced workers, that they may learn how to work. Let them seek God most earnestly. These may do a good work in canvassing if they will obey the words: 'Take heed unto thyself, and unto the doctrine.' 1 Timothy 4:16. Those who give evidence that they are truly converted, and who take up the canvassing work, will see that it is the best preparation for other lines of missionary labor.

If those who know the truth would practice it, methods would be devised for meeting the people where they are. It was the providence of God which in the beginning of the Christian church scattered the saints abroad, sending them out of Jerusalem into many parts of the world. The disciples of Christ did not stay in Jerusalem or in the cities nearby, but they went beyond the limits of their own country into the great thoroughfares of travel, seeking for the lost that they might bring them to God. Today the Lord desires to see His work carried forward in many places. We must not confine our labors to a few localities. – *Testimonies*, vol. 6, pp. 329, 330. (1900)

Two and Two. – Canvassers should be sent out two and two. Inexperienced workers should be sent out with those of more experience, who can give them help. They can converse together and study the word of life together, praying with and for each other. Thus both the younger and the elder Christian will receive the blessing of God. – *Manual for Canvassers*, p. 17. (1902)

In the Service of God. – Canvassers should be impressed with the fact that the canvassing work is the very work the Lord desires them to do. They should remember that they are in the service of God.

Painstaking effort is required; instruction must be given; a sense of the importance of the work must be kept before the workers. All must cherish the spirit of self-denial and self-sacrifice that has been exemplified in the life of our Redeemer.

Sixth of Isaiah. – Let the canvassers read the sixth chapter of Isaiah, and take its lesson home to their hearts:

'Then said I, Woe is me! for I am undone; because I am a man of unclean lips, and I dwell in the midst of a people of unclean lips: for mine eyes have seen the King, the Lord of hosts. Then flew one of the seraphims unto me, having a live coal in his hand, which he had taken with the tongs from off the altar: and he laid it upon my mouth, and said, Lo, this hath touched thy lips; and thine iniquity is taken away, and thy sin purged. Also I heard the voice of the Lord, saying, Whom shall I send, and who will go for Us? Then said I, Here am I; send me.' Isaiah 6:5-8.

This representation will be acted over and over again. The Lord desires to have many take part in this grand work, those who are consecrated, whose hearts are humble, and who are willing to engage in any line that demands their service. – *Manual for Canvassers*, pp. 18, 19. (1902)

Constantly Improving. – The follower of Jesus should be constantly improving in manners, in habits, in spirit, in labor. This is done by keeping the eye, not on mere outward, superficial attainments, but on Jesus. A transformation takes place in mind, in spirit, in character. The Christian is educated in the school of Christ to cherish the graces of His Spirit in all meekness and lowliness. He is fitting for the society of heavenly angels. – *Gospel Workers*, p. 283. (1915)

God desires us to make use of every opportunity for securing a preparation for His work. He expects us to put all our energies into its performance, and to keep our hearts alive to its sacredness and its fearful responsibilities. – *The Ministry of Healing*, p. 498. (1905)

CHAPTER 9

Exemplary in habit, deportment and dress

A High and Elevating Work. – The canvassing work is God's means of reaching many that would not otherwise be impressed with the truth. The work is a good one, the object high and elevating; and there should be a corresponding dignity of deportment. The canvasser will meet men of varied minds. He will meet those who are ignorant and debased and can appreciate nothing that does not bring them money. These will be abusive, but he should not heed them. His good nature should never fail; he should take a cheerful, hopeful view of every perplexity. He will meet those who are bereaved, disheartened, and sore and wounded in spirit. He will have many opportunities of speaking to these kind words and words of courage, hope, and faith. He may be a wellspring to refresh others if he will; but, in order to do this, he must himself draw from the Fountain of living truth. – *Testimonies*, vol. 5, p. 405. (1885)

Dangerous to Do Careless Work. – Well may everyone feel an individual responsibility in this work. Well may he consider how he may best arrest the attention, for his manner of presenting the truth may decide the destiny of a soul. If he makes a favorable impression, his influence may be to that soul a savor of life unto life; and that one person, enlightened in regard to the truth, may enlighten many others. Therefore it is dangerous to do careless work in dealing with minds. – *Testimonies*, vol. 5, p. 405. (1885)

Need of Energy and Enthusiasm. – Among the people professing present truth there is not a missionary spirit corresponding with our faith. The ring of the true gold in character is wanting. Christian life is more than they take it to be. It does not consist in mere gentleness, patience, meekness, and kindliness. These graces are essential; but there is need of courage, force, energy, and perseverance also. Many who engage in the work of canvassing are weak, nerveless, spiritless, easily discouraged. They lack push. They have not those positive traits of character that give men power to do something, – the spirit and energy that kindle enthusiasm. The canvasser is engaged in an honorable business, and he should not act as though he were ashamed of it. If he would have success attend his efforts he must be courageous and hopeful.

Cultivate Active Virtues. – The active virtues must be cultivated as well as the passive. The Christian, while he is ever ready to give the soft answer that turneth away wrath, must possess the courage of a hero to resist evil. With the charity that endureth all things, he must have the force of character which will make his influence a positive power for good. Faith must be wrought into his character. His principles must be firm; he must be noble-spirited, above all suspicion of meanness. The canvasser must not be self-inflated. As he associates with men he must not make himself conspicuous, talking of himself in a boastful way; for by this course he would disgust intelligent, sensible people. He must not be selfish in his habits nor overbearing and domineering in his manners.

Employ Tact. – Very many have settled it in their minds that they cannot find time to read one in ten thousand of the books that are published and put upon the market. And in many cases when the canvasser makes known his business, the door of the heart closes firmly; hence the great need of doing his work with tact and in a humble, prayerful spirit. He should be familiar with the word of God and have words at his command to unfold the precious truth and to show the great value of the pure reading matter he carries. – *Testimonies*, vol. 5, pp. 404, 405. (1885)

Honesty and Integrity. – The worker who has the cause of God at heart will not insist on receiving the highest wages. He will not plead, as some of our youth have done, that unless he can make a stylish and elegant appearance, and board at the best hotels, he will not be patronized. What the canvasser needs is not the faultless apparel, or the address of the dandy or the clown, but that honesty and integrity of character which is reflected in the countenance. Kindness and gentleness leave their impress upon the face, and the practiced eye sees no deception, detects no pomposity of manner.

A large number have entered the field as canvassers with whom premiums are the only means of success. They have no real merit as workers. They have no experience in practical religion; they have the same faults, the same tastes and self-indulgences, that characterized them before they claimed to be Christians. Of them it may be said that God is not in their thoughts; He has no abiding place in their hearts. There is a littleness, an earthliness, a debasement in their character and deportment, that testifies against them that they are walking in the way of their own hearts and in the sight of their own eyes. They will not practice self-denial, but are determined to enjoy life. The heavenly treasure has no attractions for them; all their tastes are downward, not upward. Friends and relatives cannot elevate such persons, for they have not a mind to despise the evil and choose the good. – *Testimonies*, vol. 5, p. 402 (1885)

Chaste, Meek, Temperate. – Canvassers need self-culture and polished manners, not the affected and artificial manners of the world, but the agreeable manners that are the natural result of kindness of heart and a desire to copy the example of Christ. They should cultivate thoughtful, caretaking habits, – habits of industry and discretion, – and should seek to honor God by making of themselves all that it is possible for them to become. Jesus made an infinite sacrifice to place them in right relations to God and to their fellow men, and divine aid combined with human effort will enable them to reach a high standard of excellence. The canvasser should be chaste like Joseph, meek like Moses, and temperate like Daniel; then a power will attend him wherever he goes. – *Testimonies*, vol. 5, p. 396. (1885)

Pleasing Dress and Manners. – We now have great

facilities for spreading the truth; but our people are not coming up to the privileges given them. They do not in every church see and feel the necessity of using their abilities in saving souls. They do not realize their duty to obtain subscribers for our periodicals, including our health journal, and to introduce our books and pamphlets. Men should be at work who are willing to be taught as to the best way of approaching individuals and families. Their dress should be neat, but not foppish, and their manners such as not to disgust the people. There is a great want of true politeness among us as a people. This should be cultivated by all who take hold of the missionary work. – *Testimonies*, vol. 4, pp. 391, 392. (1880)

Untidiness in dress brings a reproach against the truth we profess to believe. You should consider that you are a representative of the Lord Jesus Christ. Let the whole life be in harmony with Bible truth. . . . This is not a matter of but little consequence; for it affects your influence over others for time and for eternity. You cannot expect the Lord to give you the fullest success in winning souls for Him unless your whole manner and appearance is of a nature that will win respect. The truth is magnified even by the impression of neatness in dress. – *Letter 336*, 1908.

Persons of uncouth manners are not fitted for this work. Men and women who possess tact, good address, keen foresight, and discriminating minds, and who feel the value of souls, are the ones who can be successful. – *Manual for Canvassers*, p. 15. (1902)

Christian Courtesy and Helpfulness. – The canvasser should make every effort in his power to let the light of truth shine forth in good works. In his discharge of duty he should shed about him the fragrance of Christian courtesy, improving every opportunity to perform acts of helpful service. He should educate himself to speak distinctly and impressively. He should learn daily in the school of the Great Teacher. Christ will surely help those who hide in Him, depending on Him for strength. – *Review and Herald*, June 16, 1903.

Carefulness in Deportment. – There must be a decided stand taken by all our ministers and by all who profess to believe the truth, in reference to the low level that some seem inclined to take in regard to their words and their deportment. These in many cases in no way correspond with the holy, sacred truths that we profess. Many feel competent to become canvassers and colporteurs who are unconverted. They never have had the transforming grace of Christ. They are not pure. They are daily living a careless, sinful life. Their practices are such as make holy angels hide their faces. We must reach a higher standard, or we will be a reproach to the cause of God and a stumbling block to sinners. – *Letter 26d*, 1887.

Example in Health Reform. – In your association with unbelievers do not allow yourselves to be swerved from right principles. If you sit at their table, eat temperately and only of food that will not confuse the mind. Keep clear of intemperance. You cannot afford to weaken your mental or physical powers, lest you become unable to discern spiritual things. Keep your mind in such a condition that God can impress it with the precious truths of His word.

Thus you will have an influence upon others. Many try

to correct the lives of others by attacking what they regard as wrong habits. They go to those whom they think in error, and point out defects, but do not put forth earnest, tactful effort in directing the mind to true principles. Such a course often fails of securing the desired results. In trying to correct others we too often arouse their combativeness, and thus do more harm than good. Do not watch others in order to point out their faults or errors. Teach by example. Let your self-denial and your victory over appetite be an illustration of obedience to right principles. Let your life bear witness to the sanctifying, ennobling influence of truth. – *Testimonies*, vol. 6, pp. 336, 337. (1900)

The Graces of the Spirit. – God, in His great love, is seeking to develop in us the precious graces of His Spirit. He permits us to encounter obstacles, persecution, and hardships, not as a curse, but as the greatest blessing of our lives. Every temptation resisted, every trial bravely borne, gives us a new experience, and advances us in the work of character building. The soul that through divine power resists temptation, reveals to the world and to the heavenly universe the efficiency of the grace of Christ. – *Thoughts From the Mount of Blessing*, p. 17. (1896)

Personal 'Atmosphere.' – Every soul is surrounded by an atmosphere of its own, – an atmosphere, it may be, charged with the life-giving power of faith, courage, and hope, and sweet with the fragrance of love. Or it may be heavy and chill with the gloom of discontent and selfishness, or poisonous with the deadly taint of cherished sin.

By the atmosphere surrounding us, every person with whom we come in contact is consciously or unconsciously affected. – *Christ's Object Lessons*, p. 339. (1900)

Character Is Power. – Character is power. The silent witness of a true, unselfish, godly life carries an almost irresistible influence. By revealing in our own life the character of Christ we co-operate with Him in the work of saving souls. It is only by revealing in our life His character that we can co-operate with Him. And the wider the sphere of our influence, the more good we may do. – *Christ's Object Lessons*, p. 340. (1900)

True as Needle to Pole. – May the Lord help everyone to improve to the utmost the talents committed to his trust. Those who work in this cause do not study their Bibles as they should. If they did, its practical teachings would have a positive bearing upon their lives. Whatever your work may be, dear brethren and sisters, do it as for the Master, and do your best. Do not overlook present golden opportunities and let your life prove a failure while you sit idly dreaming of ease and success in a work for which God has never fitted you. Do the work that is nearest you. Do it, even though it may be amid perils and hardships in the missionary field; but do not, I beg of you, complain of hardships and self-sacrifices. Look at the Waldenses. See what plans they devised that the light of the gospel might shine into benighted minds. We should not labor with the expectation of receiving our reward in this life, but with our eyes fixed steadfastly upon the prize at the end of the race. Men and women are wanted now who are as true to duty as the needle to the pole, men and women who will work without having their way smoothed and every obstacle removed.

When You Live Your Faith. – I have described what canvassers ought to be; and may the Lord open their minds to comprehend this subject in its length and breadth, and may they realize their duty to represent the character of Christ by their patience, courage, and steadfast integrity. Let them remember that they can deny Him by a loose, lax, undecided character. Young men, if you take these principles with you into the canvassing field you will be respected; and many will believe the truth you advocate, because you live your faith, because your daily life is as a bright light set upon a candlestick, which giveth light to all that are in the house. Even your enemies, as much as they war against your doctrines, will respect you; and when you have gained this much, your simple words will have a power and will carry conviction to hearts. – *Testimonies*, vol. 5, pp. 406, 407. (1885)

CHAPTER 10

Pleasing in voice and speech

The Gift of Speech. – Of all the gifts that God has bestowed upon men, none is more precious than the gift of speech. If sanctified by the Holy Spirit, it is a power for good. It is with the tongue that we convince and persuade; with it we offer prayer and praise to God; and with it we convey rich thoughts of the Redeemer's love. By a right use of the gift of speech the canvasser can sow the precious seeds of truth in many hearts. – *Testimonies*, vol. 6, p. 337. (1900)

More attention should be given to the culture of the voice. We may have knowledge, but unless we know how to use the voice correctly, our work will be a failure. Unless we can clothe our ideas in appropriate language, of what avail is our education? Knowledge will be of little advantage to us unless we cultivate the talent of speech; but it is a wonderful power when combined with the ability to speak wise, helpful words, and to speak them in a way that will command attention. – *Testimonies*, vol. 6, p. 380. (1900)

Young men and young women, has God placed in your hearts a desire to do service for Him? Then by all means cultivate the voice to the utmost of your ability so that you can make plain the precious truth to others. – *Testimonies*, vol. 6, p. 383. (1900)

Speak Clearly and Distinctly. – When you speak, let every word be full and well rounded, every sentence clear and distinct to the very last word. Many as they approach the end of a sentence lower the tone of the voice, speaking so indistinctly that the force of the thought is destroyed. Words that are worth speaking at all are worth speaking in a clear, distinct voice, with emphasis and expression. But never search for words that will give the impression that you are learned. The greater your simplicity, the better will your words be understood. – *Testimonies*, vol. 6, p. 383. (1900)

An Indispensable Qualification. – The canvasser who can speak clearly and distinctly about the merits of the book he is introducing, will find this a great help to him in securing a subscription. He may have opportunity to read a chapter; and by the music of his voice and the emphasis placed on the words, he can make the scene presented stand out as clearly before the mind of the listener as if it could in reality be seen.

The ability to speak clearly and distinctly, in full, round tones, is invaluable in any line of work. This qualification is indispensable in those who desire to become ministers, evangelists, Bible workers, or canvassers. Those who are planning to enter these lines should be taught to use the voice in such a way that when they speak to people about the truth, it will make a decided impression for good. The truth must not be marred by being communicated through defective utterance. – *Manual for Canvassers*, pp. 23, 24. (1902)

Tell Them With Simplicity. – Men and women are wandering in the mist and fog of error. They want to know what is truth. Tell them, not in high-flown language, but with the simplicity of the children of God. – *Manual for Canvassers*, pp. 39, 40. (1902)

Words Well Chosen. – Do not, because you are among unbelievers, become careless in your words; for they are taking your measure. Study the instruction given to Nadab and Abihu, the sons of Aaron. They 'offered strange fire before the Lord, which He commanded them not.' Taking common fire they placed it upon their censers. 'And there went out fire from the Lord, and devoured them, and they died before the Lord. Then Moses said unto Aaron, This is it that the Lord spake, saying, I will be sanctified in them that come nigh Me, and before all the people I will be glorified.' Leviticus 10:1-3. Canvassers should remember that they are working with the Lord to save souls, and that they are to bring no commonness or cheapness into His sacred service. Let the mind be filled with pure, holy thoughts, and let the words be well chosen. Hinder not the success of your work by uttering light, careless words. – *Manual for Canvassers*, p. 24. (1902)

Winning Words; Gentle, Courteous Demeanor. – Those who work for Christ are to be upright and trustworthy, firm as a rock to principle, and at the same time kind and courteous. Courtesy is one of the graces of the Spirit. To deal with human minds is the greatest work ever given to man; and he who would find access to hearts must heed the injunction, 'Be pitiful, be courteous.' Love will do that which argument will fail to accomplish. But a moment's petulance, a single gruff answer, a lack of Christian politeness and courtesy in some small matter, may result in the loss of both friends and influence.

What Christ was on this earth, the Christian worker should strive to be. He is our example, not only in His spotless purity, but in His patience, gentleness, and winsomeness of disposition. His life is an illustration of true courtesy. He had ever a kind look and a word of comfort for the needy and the oppressed. His presence brought a purer atmosphere into the home. His life was as leaven working amid the elements of society. Pure and undefiled, He walked among the thoughtless, the rude, the uncourteous; among unjust publicans, unrighteous Samaritans, heathen soldiers, rough peasants, and the mixed multitude. . . .

The religion of Jesus softens whatever is hard and rough in the temper, and smooths whatever is rugged and sharp in the manners. It makes the words gentle and the demeanor winning. Let us learn from Christ how to combine a high sense of purity and integrity with sunniness of disposition. A kind, courteous Christian is the most powerful argument that can be produced in favor of Christianity.

Kind words are as dew and gentle showers to the soul. The Scripture says of Christ, that grace was poured into His lips, that He might 'know how to speak a word in season to him that is weary.' And the Lord bids us, 'Let your speech be alway with grace' 'that it may minister grace unto the hearers.'

Some with whom you are brought in contact may be rough and uncourteous, but do not, because of this, be less courteous yourself. He who wishes to preserve his own self-respect must be careful not to wound needlessly the self-respect of others. This rule should be sacredly observed toward the dullest, the most blundering. – *Gospel Workers*, pp. 121, 122. (1915)

The Saviour's Voice. – The Saviour's voice was as music to the ears of those who had been accustomed to the monotonous, spiritless preaching of the scribes and Pharisees. He spoke slowly and impressively, emphasizing those words to which He wished His hearers to give special heed. . . . The power of speech is of great value, and the voice should be cultivated for the blessing of those with whom we come in contact. – *Counsels to Parents, Teachers, and Students*, p. 240. (1913)

His Words Drew Hearts. – We should speak of Christ to those who know Him not. We should do as Christ did. Wherever He was, in the synagogue, by the wayside, in the boat thrust out a little from the land, at the Pharisee's feast or the table of the publican, He spoke to men of the things pertaining to the higher life. The things of nature, the events of daily life, were bound up by Him with the words of truth. The hearts of His hearers were drawn to Him; for He had healed their sick, had comforted their sorrowing ones, and had taken their children in His arms and blessed them. When He opened His lips to speak, their attention was riveted upon Him, and every word was to some soul a savor of life unto life.

So it should be with us. Wherever we are, we should watch for opportunities of speaking to others of the Saviour. If we follow Christ's example in doing good, hearts will open to us as they did to Him. Not abruptly, but with tact born of divine love, we can tell them of Him who is the 'Chiefest among ten thousand,' and the One 'altogether lovely.' Song of Solomon 5:10, 16. This is the very highest work in which we can employ the talent of speech. It was given to us that we might present Christ as the sin-pardoning Saviour. – *Christ's Object Lessons*, pp. 338, 339. (1900)

CHAPTER 11

Diligent in service

Energy and Willingness. – Success depends not so much on talent as on energy and willingness. It is not the possession of splendid talents that enables us to render acceptable service; but the conscientious performance of daily duties, the contented spirit, the unaffected, sincere interest in the welfare of others. In the humblest lot true excellence may be found. The commonest tasks, wrought with loving faithfulness, are beautiful in God's sight. – *Prophets and Kings*, p. 219. (1916)

No Place for Indolence. – Let no one think that he is at liberty to fold his hands and do nothing. That anyone can be saved in indolence and inactivity is an utter impossibility. Think of what Christ accomplished during His earthly ministry. How earnest, how untiring, were His efforts! He allowed nothing to turn Him aside from the work given Him. Are we following in His footsteps? He gave up all to carry out God's plan of mercy for the fallen race. In the fulfillment of the purpose of heaven, He became obedient unto death, even the death of the cross. He had had no communion with sin, had known nothing of it; but He came to this world, and took upon His sinless soul the guilt of sinful man, that sinners might stand justified before God. He grappled with temptation, overcoming in our behalf. The Son of God, pure and unsullied, bore the penalty of transgression, and received the stroke of death that brought deliverance to the race. – *Review and Herald*, Jan. 20, 1903.

Wholehearted Labor. – God's servants are to be 'not slothful in business; fervent in spirit; serving the Lord.' Listlessness and inefficiency are not piety. When we realize that we are working for God, we shall have a higher sense than we have ever had before of the sacredness of spiritual service. This realization will put life and vigilance and persevering energy into the discharge of every duty. Religion, pure, undefiled religion, is intensely practical. Nothing but earnest, wholehearted labor will avail in the saving of souls. We are to make our everyday duties acts of devotion, constantly increasing in usefulness because we see our work in the light of eternity. *Letter 43*, 1902.

Regularity and Dispatch. – God has no use for lazy men in His cause; He wants thoughtful, kind, affectionate, earnest workers. . . . Persons who have not acquired habits of close industry and economy of time should have set rules to prompt them to regularity and dispatch. – *Testimonies*, vol. 4, p. 411. (1880)

Rise Early, Work Industriously. – The work of the colporteur is elevating and will prove a success if he is honest, earnest, and patient, steadily pursuing the work he has undertaken. His heart must be in the work. He must rise early and work industriously, putting to proper use the faculties God has given him. Difficulties must be met.

If confronted with unceasing perseverance, they will be overcome. The worker may continually be forming a symmetrical character. Great characters are formed by little acts and efforts. – *Manual for Canvassers*, p. 18. (1902)

Faithful to Duty. – Those who have entered the canvassing field are in danger of not feeling the necessity of being particular in their work. They are in danger of becoming content with superficial attainments, of being careless in their manners and lazy in mind. There should be faithful discharge of duty in the canvassing field, for it is important and sacred. – *Review and Herald*, May 20, 1890.

Exact and Diligent. – Remember that in whatever position you may serve, you are revealing motive, developing character. Whatever your work, do it with exactness, with diligence; overcome the inclination to seek an easy task. – *The Ministry of Healing*, p. 499. (1905)

When we labor diligently for the salvation of our fellow men, God will prosper our every effort. – *Testimonies*, vol. 9, p. 86. (1909)

When the canvasser enters upon his work, he should not allow himself to be diverted, but should intelligently keep to the point with all diligence. And yet, while he is doing his canvassing, he should not be heedless of opportunities to help souls who are seeking for light and who need the consolation of the Scriptures. If the canvasser walks with God, if he prays for heavenly wisdom that he may do good and only good in his labor, he will be quick to discern his opportunities and the needs of the souls with whom he comes in contact. He will make the most of every opportunity for drawing souls to Christ. In the spirit of Christ he will be ready to speak a word to him that is weary. – *Testimonies*, vol. 6, p. 339. (1900)

Report Encouraging Experience. – Let those who gain such an experience in working for the Lord write an account of it for our papers, that others may be encouraged. Let the canvasser tell of the joy and blessing he has received in his ministry as an evangelist. These reports should find a place in our papers, for they are far-reaching in their influence. They will be as sweet fragrance in the church, a savor of life unto life. Thus it is seen that God works with those who co-operate with Him. – *Testimonies*, vol. 6, p. 336. (1900)

CHAPTER 12

Given to much prayer

Pray for a Deeper Experience. – To our canvassers, to all whom God has entrusted with talents that they may co-operate with Him, I would say: Pray, oh, pray for a deeper experience. Go forth with your hearts softened and subdued by a study of the precious truths that God has given us for this time. Drink deeply of the water of salvation, that it may be in your hearts as a living spring, flowing forth to refresh souls ready to perish. God will then give wisdom to enable you to impart aright. He will make you channels for communicating His blessings. He will help you to reveal His attributes by imparting to others the wisdom and understanding that He has imparted to you.

I pray the Lord that you may understand this subject in its length and breadth and depth, and that you may feel your responsibility to represent the character of Christ by patience, by courage, and by steadfast integrity. 'And the peace of God, which passeth all understanding, shall guard your hearts and your thoughts in Christ Jesus.' Philippians 4:7, R.V. – *Testimonies*, vol. 6, p. 320. (1900)

Pray Humbly and Fervently. – Humble, fervent prayer would do more in behalf of the circulation of our books than all the expensive embellishments in the world. If the workers will turn their attention to that which is true and living and real; if they will pray for, believe for, and trust in the Holy Spirit, His power will be poured upon them in strong, heavenly currents, and right and lasting impressions will be made upon the human heart. Then pray and work, and work and pray, and the Lord will work with you. – *Testimonies*, vol. 6, p. 319. (1900)

Satan is on your track. He is an artful opponent, and the malignant spirit which you meet in your work is inspired by him. Those whom he controls echo his words. If the veil could be rent away from their eyes, those thus worked would see Satan plying all his arts to win them from the truth. In rescuing souls from his devices, far more will be accomplished by Christlike, humble prayer than by many words without prayer.

Pray Constantly. – The workers should keep the soul constantly uplifted to God in prayer. They are never alone. If they have faith in God, if they realize that to them is committed the work of giving to the people light on Bible subjects, they constantly enjoy the companionship of Christ. – *Manual for Canvassers*, p. 40. (1902)

Power in Importunate Prayer. – Jacob prevailed because he was persevering and determined. His experience testifies to the power of importunate prayer. It is now that we are to learn this lesson of prevailing prayer, of unyielding faith. The greatest victories to the church of Christ or to the individual Christian, are not those that are gained by talent or education, by wealth, or the favor of men. They are those victories that are gained in the audience chamber with God, when earnest, agonizing faith lays hold upon the mighty arm of power.

Those who are unwilling to forsake every sin and to seek earnestly for God's blessing, will not obtain it. But all who will lay hold of God's promises as did Jacob, and be as earnest and persevering as he was, will succeed as he succeeded. – *Patriarchs and Prophets*, p. 203. (1890)

Every Difficulty a Call to Prayer. – The path of sincerity and integrity is not a path free from obstruction, but in every difficulty we are to see a call to prayer. – *The Desire of Ages*, p. 667. (1898)

Prayer and Bible Study Essential. – Satan well knows that all whom he can lead to neglect prayer and the searching of the Scriptures, will be overcome by his attacks. Therefore he invents every possible device to engross the mind. – *The Great Controversy*, p. 519. (1888)

Those who will put on the whole armor of God and devote some time every day to meditation and prayer and to the study of the Scriptures will be connected with heaven and will have a saving, transforming influence upon those around them. – *Testimonies*, vol. 5, p. 112. (1882)

Praying With People. – There are many, who, because of prejudice, will never know the truth unless it is brought to their homes. The canvasser may find these souls and minister to them. There is a line of work in house-to-house labor which he can accomplish more successfully than others. He can become acquainted with the people and understand their true necessities; he can pray with them and can point them to the Lamb of God that taketh away the sin of the world. Thus the way will be opened for the special message for this time to find access to their hearts. – *Testimonies*, vol. 6, p. 314. (1900)

By Prayer and Song. – The work of the canvasser evangelist, whose heart is imbued with the Holy Spirit, is fraught with wonderful possibilities for good. The presentation of the truth, in love and simplicity, from house to house, is in harmony with the instruction that Christ gave His disciples when He sent them out on their first missionary tour. By songs of praise, by humble, heartfelt prayers, many will be reached. The divine Worker will be present to send conviction to hearts. 'I am with you alway,' is His promise. With the assurance of the abiding presence of such a helper we may labor with faith and hope and courage. – *Testimonies*, vol. 9, p. 34. (1909)

God Gives Success. – It is God alone who can give success either in preparing or in circulating our publications. If in faith we maintain His principles, He will co-operate with us in placing the books in the hands of those whom they will benefit. The Holy Spirit is to be prayed for, trusted in, believed in. Humble, fervent prayer will do more to promote the circulation of our books than will all the expensive ornamentation in the world. – *Testimonies*, vol. 7, pp. 158, 159. (1902)

The colporteur evangelist in action

CHAPTER 13

Points on selling

Introducing Our Books. – Other publishers have regular systems of introducing into the market books of no vital interest. 'The children of this world are in their generation wiser than the children of light.' Golden opportunities occur almost daily where the silent messengers of truth might be introduced into families and to individuals; but no advantage is taken of these opportunities by the indolent, thoughtless ones. Living preachers are few. There is only one where there should be a hundred. Many are making a great mistake in not putting their talents to use in seeking to save the souls of their fellow men.

Hundreds of men should be engaged in carrying the light all through our cities, villages, and towns. The public mind must be agitated. God says: Let light be sent out into all parts of the field. He designs that men shall be channels of light, bearing it to those who are in darkness. – *Testimonies*, vol. 4, p. 389. (1880)

Canvassing campaigns are to be organized for the sale of our literature, that the world may be enlightened as to what is just before us. – *Review and Herald*, June 2, 1903.

Circulation Increases Demand. – Our publishing houses should show marked prosperity. Our people can sustain them if they will show a decided interest to work our publications into the market. . . . The wider the circulation of our publications, the greater will be the demand for books that make plain the Scriptures of truth. Many are becoming disgusted with the inconsistencies, the errors, and the apostasy of the churches, and with the festivals, fairs, lotteries, and numerous inventions to extort money for church purposes. There are many who are seeking for light in the darkness. If our papers, tracts, and books, expressing the truth in plain Bible language, could be widely circulated, many would find that they are just what they want. But many of our brethren act as though the people were to come to them or send to our offices to obtain publications, when thousands do not know that they exist.

Exalt the Value of the Books. – God calls upon His people to act like living men and not to be indolent, sluggish, and indifferent. We must carry the publications to the people and urge them to accept, showing them that they will receive much more than their money's worth. Exalt the value of the books you offer. You cannot regard them too highly. – *Testimonies*, vol. 4, p. 392. (1880)

Prices of Our Publications. – Some things of grave importance have not been receiving due attention at our offices of publication. Men in responsible positions should have worked up plans whereby our books could be circulated and not lie on the shelves, falling dead from the press. Our people are behind the times and are not following the opening providence of God.

Many of our publications have been thrown into the market at so low a figure that the profits are not sufficient to sustain the office and keep good a fund for continual use. And those of our people who have no special burden of the various branches of the work . . . do not become informed in regard to the wants of the cause and the capital required to keep the business moving. They do not understand the liability to losses and the expense every day occurring to such institutions. They seem to think that everything moves off without much care or outlay of means, and therefore they will urge the necessity of the lowest figures on our publications, thus leaving scarcely any margin.

And after the prices have been reduced to almost ruinous figures, they manifest but a feeble interest in increasing the sales of the very books on which they have asked such low prices. The object gained, their burden ceases, when they ought to have an earnest interest and a real care to press the sale of the publications, thereby sowing the seeds of truth and bringing means into the offices to invest in other publications.

There has been a very great neglect of duty on the part of ministers in not interesting the churches in the localities where they labor, in regard to this matter. When once the prices of books are reduced, it is a very difficult matter to get them again upon a paying basis, as men of narrow minds will cry, Speculation, not discerning that no one man is benefited, and that God's instrumentalities must not be crippled for want of capital. Books that ought to be widely circulated are lying useless in our offices of publication because there is not interest enough manifested to get them circulated.

The press is a power; but if its products fall dead for

want of men who will execute plans to widely circulate them, its power is lost. While there has been a quick foresight to discern the necessity of laying out means in facilities to multiply books and tracts, plans to bring back the means invested so as to produce other publications, have been neglected. The power of the press, with all its advantages, is in their hands; and they can use it to the very best account, or they can be half asleep and through inaction lose the advantages which they might gain. By judicious calculation they can extend the light in the sale of books and pamphlets. They can send them into thousands of families that now sit in the darkness of error. – *Testimonies*, vol. 4, pp. 388, 389. (1880)

Not to Rely on Premiums. – Those who have genuine humility, and whose minds have been expanded by the truths unfolded in the gospel, will have an influence that will be felt. They will make an impression upon minds and hearts, and they will be respected by the larger number, even of those who have no sympathy with their faith. With the truths of the Bible and our valuable papers they will have success, for the Lord will open the way before them. But to urge our papers upon the people by means of gifts and premiums does not have a permanent influence for good. If our workers would go forth relying upon the truths of the Bible, with the love of Christ and of souls in their hearts, they would accomplish more in obtaining permanent subscribers than by depending upon premiums or low prices. The prominence given to these inducements to take the paper gives the impression that it cannot possess real merit in itself. The results would be better if the paper were made prominent and the money spent for premiums were reserved to distribute a few copies free. When premiums are offered, some may be induced to take the paper who otherwise would not, but others will refuse to subscribe because they think it a speculation. If the canvasser would present the merits of the paper itself, with his heart uplifted to God for success, and would depend less upon premiums, more would be accomplished. – *Testimonies*, vol. 5, p. 401. (1885)

Canvassers should be secured to handle the books, *Great Controversy, Patriarchs and Prophets, Desire of Ages, Daniel and the Revelation*, and other books of like character, who have a sense of the value of the matter these books contain, and a realization of the work to be done to interest people in the truth. Special help, which is above all the supposed advantages of illustrations, will be given to such canvassers. The canvassers who are born again by the work of the Holy Spirit, will be accompanied by angels, who will go before them to the dwellings of the people, preparing the way for them. – *Manuscript 131*, 1899.

Open Doors by Courtesy and Kindness. – One of the simplest, yet most effective methods of labor is that of the canvasser evangelist. By courteous behavior and kindness such a worker may open the door of many homes. When he is entertained by strangers he should show himself thoughtful and helpful. Never should he make himself a burden, requiring to be waited upon by those upon whom rest the cares of the household. Should there be sickness in the home while he is there, let him do all he can to help. Sometimes he will find men who say they are too busy to listen to a canvass or a Bible reading. Often he may gain their attention by helping them in their work. – *Manuscript 26*, 1905.

Win Confidence by Helpfulness. – When staying at the homes of the people, share the burdens of the household. . . . Help the tired father do the chores. Take an interest in the children. Be considerate. Work in humility, and the Lord will work with you. – *Review and Herald*, Nov. 11, 1902.

In every place that you visit, you will find the sick and suffering. Relieve them if possible, even if by so doing, you are detained some little time. . . . The use of simple means in the treatment of the sick will be an object lesson. If at all consistent, pray for the sick one. God may raise him up, and this will be a witness for the truth. Tell the families you visit what they must do to keep well. Take with you some pamphlets bearing on health reform, and leave them with the people. Thus you can sow the seeds of truth. – *Manuscript 18a*, 1901.

Simple Treatments. – Canvassers should be able to give instruction in regard to the treatment of the sick. They should learn the simple methods of hygienic treatment. Thus they may work as medical missionaries, ministering to the souls and the bodies of the suffering. This work should now be going forward in all parts of the world. Thus multitudes might be blessed by the prayers and instruction of God's servants. – *Testimonies*, vol. 6, p. 324.

Show Value of Healthful Living. – Canvassers should never forget that they are to make earnest efforts to do medical missionary work. The publications treating on health reform are now very much needed by the world. Intemperance is striving for the mastery. Self-indulgence is increasing. In his work the canvasser can do much to show those whom he visits the value of healthful living. Instead of staying at a hotel, he should, if possible, obtain lodging with a private family. As he sits at the meal table with the family, let him practice the instruction given in the health works he is selling. If he has opportunity, let him speak of the value of health reform. If in word and action he is courteous, he will find that his words leave an impression for good. – *Manuscript 113,* 1901.

Call Attention to Health Literature. – Tell the people that you have for sale books which give much valuable instruction regarding sickness and disease and how to avoid them, and that a study of this instruction saves much suffering and saves also much of the money spent in paying doctor's bills. Tell them that in these books is advice which they cannot possibly obtain from their physician during the short visits he makes. – *Manuscript 113,* 1901.

'Your feet shod with the preparation of the gospel of peace,' you will be prepared to walk from house to house, carrying the truth to the people. Sometimes you will find it very trying to do work of this kind; but if you go forth in faith, the Lord will go before you, and His light will shine upon your pathway. As you enter the homes of your neighbors to sell or to give away our literature, and in humility to teach them the truth, you will be accompanied by the light of heaven. Learn to sing the simplest of songs. These will help you in house-to-house labor, and hearts will be touched by the influence of the Holy Spirit. . . . We may enjoy the companionship of the heavenly angels. We may not discern their forms, but by faith we may know that they are with us. – *Review and Herald,* Nov. 11, 1902.

The Real Purpose. – By many of our canvassers there has been a departure from right principles. Through a desire to reap worldly advantage their minds have been drawn away from the real purpose and spirit of the work. Let none think that display will make a right impression upon the people. This will not secure the best or most permanent results. Our work is to direct minds to the solemn truths for this time. It is only when our own hearts are imbued with the spirit of the truths contained in the book we are selling, and when in humility we call the attention of the people to these truths, that real success will attend our efforts; for it is only then that the Holy Spirit, who convinces of sin, of righteousness, and of judgment, will be present to impress hearts. – *Testimonies,* vol. 6, pp. 318, 319. (1900)

CHAPTER 14

The colporteur evangelist and finance

Prompt Payment for Books. – The work is halting because gospel principles are not obeyed by those who claim to be following Christ. The loose way in which some canvassers, both old and young, have performed their work shows that they have important lessons to learn. Much haphazard work has been presented before me. Some have trained themselves in deficient habits, and this deficiency has been brought into the work of God. The tract and missionary societies [Book and Bible Houses] have been deeply involved in debt through the failure of canvassers to meet their indebtedness. Canvassers have felt that they were ill-treated if required to pay promptly for the books received from the publishing houses. Yet to require prompt remittal is the only way to carry on business.

Absolute Honesty. – Matters should be so arranged that canvassers shall have enough to live on without overdrawing. This door of temptation must be closed and barred. However honest a canvasser may be, circumstances will arise in his work which will be to him a sore temptation.

Laziness and indolence are not the fruit borne upon the Christian tree. No soul can practice prevarication or dishonesty in handling the Lord's goods and stand guiltless before God. All who do this are in action denying Christ. While they profess to keep and teach God's law, they fail to maintain its principles.

No Reckless Spending. – The Lord's goods should be handled with faithfulness. The Lord has entrusted men with life and health and reasoning powers. He has given them physical and mental strength to be exercised; and should not these gifts be faithfully and diligently employed to His name's glory? Have our brethren considered that they must give an account for all the talents placed in their possession? Have they traded wisely with their Lord's goods, or have they spent His substance recklessly, and are they written in heaven as unfaithful servants? Many are spending their Lord's money in riotous enjoyment, so called; they are not gaining an experience of self-denial, but spending money on vanities, and are failing to bear the cross after Jesus. Many who were privileged with precious, God-given opportunities have wasted their lives and are now found in suffering and want.

God calls for decided improvement to be made in the various branches of the work. The business done in connection with the cause of God must be marked with greater precision and exactness. There has not been firm, decided effort to bring about essential reform. – *Testimonies*, vol. 6, pp. 337,338. (1900)

Not to Incur Debt. – All must practice economy. No worker should manage his affairs in a way to incur debt. The practice of drawing money from the treasury before it is earned, is a snare. In this way the resources are limited, so that laborers cannot be supported in missionary work. When one voluntarily becomes involved in debt, he is entangling himself in one of Satan's nets which he sets for souls. – *Manual for Canvassers*, p. 65. (1902)

Canvassers Who Expect to Be Helped. – When they get into difficulty, some canvassers expect that money is to be drawn from the treasury to help them out, only to get into strait places again, and again to require help. Those who are stewards of the means in the treasury must keep a sharp lookout to see that the supply is not exhausted by these drafts. When men cannot by canvassing bring into the treasury every dollar that belongs to it rightly, let them stop just where they are. They should not engage in canvassing unless they can bring means into the treasury, instead of robbing it. – *Manual for Canvassers*, p. 65. (1902)

Truthful, Honest, and Faithful. – The canvassing work is not to be conducted in a slack, loose manner. Those engaged in work that calls for the handling of money should keep a strict account of every penny received and paid out. The education in accuracy thus gained will fit them for greater usefulness.

If a canvasser continues to order books, and sends no report of his work, making no statement regarding their delivery and the receipt and expenditure of the money that he handles, those in charge of the work should, in a kind, friendly manner, endeavor to ascertain the true situation. To supply books freely to an agent until he is hopelessly involved in debt is to do injustice both to the canvasser and to those by whom he is employed. Such a loose, careless way of working brings discouragement.

A worker who sees that he is unable to make a success of the canvassing work should go to the proper persons and tell them that he cannot continue in that line of work.

Every canvasser should be truthful, honest, and faithful. How many souls might be saved from temptation, and how much sorrow might be avoided, if all our workers were trained to be as true as steel to principle! – *Manuscript 20*, 1904.

Results of Careless Financial Habits. – Some canvassers have conducted their business in such a slack, loose way as to be constantly sapping the funds needed for carrying on the work. They have sold books, and given the impression that they were working for the cause; but instead of bringing in the means so much needed to advance the work, they have taken many dollars from the treasury. The means which came into their hands, which was not their own, they appropriated to defray their own expenses, the expenses of their families, or to favor their family connections.

By appropriating to their own use that which belongs to the cause of God, canvassers involve themselves in difficulties, separate their souls from God, and create a feeling of uncertainty, a want of confidence in those who are laboring with them in the field. At the same time they do injustice to their fellow laborers. Men who do their very best are liable to be regarded with suspicion, and thus are made to suffer because of the course of untrustworthy persons.

The result is that the cause of God is involved in

perplexity and brought into embarrassment, and a heavy burden is cast upon those who were appointed to bear weighty responsibilities. If this loose way of doing business is permitted to continue, it will not only drain the treasury of means, but will cut off the supplies that flow from the people. It will destroy their confidence in those at the head of the work who have the management of funds, and will lead many to discontinue their gifts and offerings.

The course of these careless workmen has brought upon men in leading positions a burden that grieves them to the heart. They are perplexed to know how they can guard the cause of God from every species of robbery, and yet save the souls of those who have such perverted ideas as to what is true honesty.

The practice of borrowing money to relieve some pressing necessity, and making no calculation for canceling the indebtedness, however common, is demoralizing. The Lord would have all who believe the truth converted from these self-deceiving practices. They should choose rather to suffer want than to commit a dishonest act. . . . If those who see the truth do not change in character corresponding to the sanctifying influence of the truth, they will be a savor of death unto death. They will misrepresent the truth, bring a reproach upon it, and dishonor Christ, who is truth.

The question to be considered is, By what means the work can be carried forward, and canvassers be prevented from embarrassing the cause, and casting a burden upon the publishing houses by a careless, selfish way of doing business. This question is of consequence. – *Manuscript 168*, 1898.

Side Lines. – Some have brought themselves and their families into most distressing circumstances through poor management in book canvassing. They have run in debt, and have borrowed money of men not of our faith.

With the work of scattering our publications and advocating the truth, some have mingled scheming, buying and selling. This makes a bad combination. As they labor to obtain advantage for themselves, they are allured by the prospect of buying things for less and selling them for more than their value. Therefore the world regards them as sharpers, men who will gain advantage for themselves without considering the case of others. They do not keep the commandments of God; for they do not love their neighbor as themselves. – *Manual for Canvassers*, p. 62. (1902)

Financial Gain Not Paramount. – If our canvassers are controlled by the spirit of financial gain, if they circulate the book upon which they can make the most money, to the neglect of others that the people need, I ask, In what sense is theirs a missionary work? Where is the missionary spirit, the spirit of self-sacrifice? The work of the intelligent, God-fearing canvasser has been represented as equal to that of the gospel minister. Then should the canvasser feel at liberty, any more than the minister, to act from selfish motives? Should he be unfaithful to the principles of missionary work, and sell only those books that are cheapest and easiest to handle, neglecting to place before the people books which will give most light, because by so doing he can earn more money for himself? How is the missionary spirit revealed here? Has not the canvassing work ceased to be what it should be? How is it that no voice is raised to correct this state of things? – *Manual for Canvassers*, pp. 47, 48. (1902)

But many are attracted into the canvassing work to sell books and pictures that do not express our faith, and do not give light to the purchaser. They are induced to do this because the financial prospects are more flattering than those that can be offered them as licentiates. These persons are obtaining no special fitness for the gospel ministry. They are not gaining that experience which would fit them for the work. They are not learning to bear the burden of souls and daily obtaining a knowledge of the most successful way of winning people to the truth. They are losing time and opportunities.

These men are frequently turned aside from the convictions of the Spirit of God, and receive a worldly stamp of character, forgetting how much they owe to the Lord, who gave His life for them. They use their powers for their own selfish interests, and refuse to labor in the vineyard of the Lord. – *Manual for Canvassers*, p. 43. (1902)

Not to Offer Special Inducements – Many of the workers in the canvassing field are making no sacrifices. As a class they have less of the missionary spirit than the workers in any other denomination. When the way is all prepared for them, when they can command the highest wages, then they are willing to enter the field. Many inducements are presented to canvassers to handle popular books; large wages are offered them; and many refuse to work for less wages to circulate books treating on present truth. Therefore the inducements have been increased to correspond with those offered by other publishers, and as a consequence the expense of getting our publications before the people is large; many of the canvassers obtain their money easily and spend it freely. – *Testimonies*, vol. 5, pp. 403, 404. (1885)

Economy and Self-Denial. – Quite a sum may be expended in hotel bills that are not at all necessary. The cause of God lay so near the heart of the pioneers in this message that they seldom took a meal at a hotel, even though the cost was but twenty-five cents each. But young men and women generally are not educated to economize, and waste follows waste everywhere. In some families there is a wicked waste of enough to support another family if reasonable economy were used. If, while traveling, our youth will keep an exact account of the money they expend, item by item, their eyes will be opened to see the leaks. While they may not be called upon to deprive themselves of warm meals, as the early workers did in their itinerant life, they may learn to supply their real wants with less expense than they now think necessary. There are persons who practice self-denial in order to give means to the cause of God; then let the workers in the cause also practice self-denial by limiting their expenses as far as possible. It would be well for all our workers to study the history of the Waldensian missionaries and to imitate their example of sacrifice and self-denial. – *Testimonies*, vol. 5, p. 400. (1885)

CHAPTER 15

Co-operating with other Gospel workers

Combine Work of Press and Preacher. The press is a powerful instrumentality which God has ordained to be combined with the energies of the living preacher to bring the truth before all nations, kindreds, tongues, and peoples. – *Life Sketches*, p. 217. (1915)

Mission of the 'Silent Messengers.' – I have been instructed that even where the people hear the message from the living preacher, the canvasser should carry on his work in co-operation with the minister; for though the minister may faithfully present the message, the people are not able to retain it all. The printed page is therefore essential, not only in awakening them to the importance of the truth for this time, but in rooting and grounding them in the truth and establishing them against deceptive error. Papers and books are the Lord's means of keeping the message for this time continually before the people. In enlightening and confirming souls in the truth the publications will do a far greater work than can be accomplished by the ministry of the word alone. The silent messengers that are placed in the homes of the people through the work of the canvasser will strengthen the gospel ministry in every way; for the Holy Spirit will impress minds as they read the books, just as He impresses the minds of those who listen to the preaching of the word. The same ministry of angels attends the books that contain the truth as attends the work of the minister. – *Testimonies*, vol. 6, pp. 315, 316. (1900)

Co-operate With Gospel Minister. – The work of co-operating with the gospel minister in carrying the present truth to all nations, tongues, and peoples, is indeed a most essential one. It should be conducted in a manner in keeping with the exalted truth which we profess to love. Through the canvassing work, the minds of many who are now absorbed in iniquity and error, may be enlightened. Through this agency a people may be prepared to stand in the great day of God which is just before us. – *Review and Herald*, May 20, 1890.

Part of Medical Work and of Ministry. – The preaching of the word is a means by which the Lord has ordained that His warning message shall be given to the world. In the Scriptures the faithful teacher is represented as a shepherd of the flock of God. He is to be respected and his work appreciated. Genuine medical missionary work is bound up with the ministry, and the canvassing work is to be a part both of the medical missionary work and of the ministry. To those who are engaged in this work I would say: As you visit the people, tell them that you are a gospel worker and that you love the Lord. – *Testimonies*, vol. 6, p. 323. (1900)

The Colporteur and Bible Work. – Letters have been received by me, making inquiries in regard to the duties of the canvasser. Some have said that in visiting the people they have found favorable opportunities for presenting the truth for this time, and have almost been forced into giving Bible readings. These opportunities they could not conscientiously neglect. On the other hand, letters come saying that our canvassers are neglecting their work in order to give Bible readings upon doctrinal subjects, and that the prejudice aroused by these readings has made it difficult for the canvasser to deliver his books; and some are asking counsel in regard to these matters.

Not to Dwell Upon Doctrinal Subjects. – We think that there is truth in both the statements, – that canvassers find favorable opportunities for leading the people to a better understanding of the Bible, and that, because of the way in which they meet these opportunities, prejudice is aroused, and the work hindered. When the canvasser enters upon his work, he should not allow himself to be diverted, but should intelligently keep to the point with all diligence. And yet while he is faithful in his canvassing, he should not neglect opportunities to help those who are seeking for light and who need the consolation of the Scriptures. If the canvasser walks with God, if he prays for heavenly wisdom that he may do good and only good in his labor, he will be quick to discern the needs of those with whom he comes in contact. He will make the most of his opportunities to draw souls to Christ, not dwelling upon doctrinal subjects, but upon the love of God, upon His mercy and goodness in the plan of salvation. In the spirit of Christ he will be ready to speak a word in season to him that is weary.

The great need of the soul is to know God and Jesus Christ, whom He has sent. The Bible abounds in practical lessons, which the canvasser may safely present. If he can by this means impart a knowledge of practical religion, he will be feeding the people, who need just such precious food. – *Manual for Canvassers*, pp. 35, 36. (1902)

Be Bible Students. – We have a grand work to do for the Master, to open the word of God to those who are in the darkness of error. Young friends, act as though you had a sacred charge. You should be Bible students, ever ready to give to every man that asketh you a reason of the hope that is in you. By your true Christian dignity give evidence that you know you have a truth that it is for the interest of the people to hear. If this truth is inwrought in the soul, it will manifest itself in the countenance and demeanor, in a calm, noble self-possession and peace which the Christian alone can possess. – *Testimonies*, vol. 5, p. 401. (1885)

Hold Bible Readings. – As the canvasser visits the people at their homes, he will often have opportunity to read to them from the Bible or from books that teach the truth. When he discovers those who are searching for truth he can hold Bible readings with them. These Bible readings are just what the people need. God will use in His service those who thus show a deep interest in perishing souls. Through them He will impart light to those who are ready to receive instruction. – *Testimonies*, vol. 6, p. 324. (1900)

Section IV

In league with the divine

CHAPTER 16

Led by God's Spirit

Under the Control of the Holy Spirit. – The canvassing work should never languish. The agencies set in operation to do this work need always to be under the control of the Holy Spirit of God. – *Letter 82, 1899.*

Man needs a power outside of and beyond himself, to restore him to the likeness of God, and enable him to do the work of God; but this does not make the human agency unessential. Humanity lays hold upon divine power, Christ dwells in the heart by faith; and through co-operation with the divine, the power of man becomes efficient for good.

He who called the fishermen of Galilee is still calling men to His service. And He is just as willing to manifest His power through us as through the first disciples. – *The Desire of Ages*, pp. 296, 297. (1898)

Pray for the Holy Spirit. – We should pray as earnestly for the descent of the Holy Spirit as the disciples prayed on the Day of Pentecost. If they needed it at that time, we need it more today. Moral darkness, like a funeral pall, covers the earth. All manner of false doctrines, heresies, and satanic deceptions are misleading the minds of men. Without the Spirit and power of God it

will be in vain that we labor to present the truth. –
Testimonies, vol. 5, p. 158. (1882)

When under test young men show that they have a
genuine burden for souls, and intense longing to save
their fellow men, they will see souls converted. From
their work a harvest for the Lord will be reaped. Let
them go out as true missionaries to do the work of circulating books containing present truth. As they go, let
their prayers ascend to God for increased light and for
the guidance of His Spirit, that they may know how to
speak a word in season. When they see an opportunity
to do an act of kindness, let them take hold as if they
were working for wages. Let them remember that thus
they are doing errands for the Lord. – *Manuscript 75*,
1900.

His Help Assured. – God does not ask us to do in our
own strength the work before us. He has provided divine
assistance for all the emergencies to which our human
resources are unequal. He gives the Holy Spirit to help in
every strait, to strengthen our hope and assurance, to il-
luminate our minds and purify our hearts. – *Testimonies*,
vol. 8, p. 19. (1904)

The humble, efficient worker who obediently responds
to the call of God may be sure of receiving divine assistance. To feel so great and holy a responsibility is of itself
elevating to the character. It calls into action the highest
mental qualities, and their continued exercise strength-
ens and purifies mind and heart. The influence upon
one's own life, as well as upon the life of others, is incal-
culable. – *Testimonies*, vol. 6, p. 340. (1900)

Holy Spirit Transforms the Life. – When the Spirit of God takes possession of the heart, it transforms the life. Sinful thoughts are put away, evil deeds are renounced; love, humility, and peace take the place of anger, envy, and strife. Joy takes the place of sadness, and the countenance reflects the light of heaven. – *The Desire of Ages*, p. 173. (1898)

The Secret of Success. – Joshua had received the promise that God would surely overthrow these enemies of Israel, yet he put forth as earnest effort as though success depended upon the armies of Israel alone. He did all that human energy could do, and then he cried in faith for divine aid. The secret of success is the union of divine power with human effort. Those who achieve the greatest results are those who rely most implicitly upon the Almighty Arm. – *Patriarchs and Prophets*, p. 509. (1890)

Take Hold of Power. – Let canvassing evangelists give themselves up to be worked by the Holy Spirit. Let them by persevering prayer take hold of the power which comes from God, trusting in Him in living faith. His great and effectual influence will be with every true, faithful worker.

As God blesses the minister and the evangelist in their earnest efforts to place the truth before the people, so He will bless the faithful canvasser. – *Testimonies*, vol. 6, p. 340. (1900)

Let young and old consecrate themselves to God, take up the work, and go forward, laboring in humility under the control of the Holy Spirit. – *Testimonies*, vol. 6, p. 331. (1900)

Realize every moment that you must have the presence

of the Holy Spirit; for it can do a work that you cannot do of yourself. – *Testimonies to Ministers*, p. 310. (1923)

Become His Instrumentality. – Our books should be handled by consecrated workers, whom the Holy Spirit can use as His instrumentalities. Christ is our sufficiency, and we are to present the truth in humble simplicity, letting it bear its own savor of life unto life. – *Testimonies*, vol. 6, p. 319. (1900)

Holy Spirit Gives Words. – Hearts cannot fail to be touched by the story of the atonement. As you learn the meekness and lowliness of Christ, you will know what you should say to the people; for the Holy Spirit will tell you what words to speak. Those who realize the necessity of keeping the heart under the control of the Holy Spirit will be enabled to sow seed that will spring up unto eternal life. This is the work of the evangelistic canvasser. – *Testimonies*, vol. 6, p. 325. (1900)

He Impresses Hearts. – The Lord Jesus standing by the side of the canvasser, walking with them, is the chief worker. If we recognize Christ as the One who is with us to prepare the way, the Holy Spirit by our side will make impressions in just the lines needed. – *Manual for Canvassers*, p. 40. (1902)

He Gives Success. – We can enlighten the people only through the power of God. The canvassers must keep their own souls in living connection with God. They should labor praying that God will open the way, and prepare hearts to receive the message He sends them. It is not the ability of the agent or worker, but it is the Spirit of God moving upon the heart that will give true success. – *Manuscript 31, 1890.*

Near to Help in Time of Need. – To all who are reaching out to feel the guiding hand of God, the moment of greatest discouragement is the time when divine help is nearest. They will look back with thankfulness upon the darkest part of their way. . . . From every temptation and every trial He will bring them forth with firmer faith and a richer experience. – *The Desire of Ages*, p. 528. (1898)

'All Power' Available. – Those in the darkness of error are the purchase of the blood of Christ. They are the fruit of His suffering, and they are to be labored for. Let our canvassers know that it is for the advancement of Christ's kingdom that they are laboring. He will teach them as they go forth to their God-appointed work, to warn the world of a soon-coming judgment. Accompanied by the power of persuasion, the power of prayer, the power of the love of God, the evangelist's work will not, cannot, be without fruit. Think of the interest that the Father and the Son have in this work. As the Father loves the Son, so the Son loves those that are His, – those who work as He worked to save perishing souls. None need feel that they are powerless; for Christ declares, 'All power is given unto Me in heaven and in earth.' He has promised that He will give this power to His workers. His power is to become their power. They are to link their souls with God. Christ desires all to enjoy the wealth of His grace, which is beyond all computation. It is limitless, exhaustless. It is ours by eternal covenant, if we will be workers together with God. It is ours if we will unite with Him to bring many sons and daughters to God. – *Review and Herald*, June 2, 1903.

Consecrate yourselves wholly to the work of God. He is your strength, and He will be at your right hand, helping you to carry on His merciful designs. – *Testimonies*, vol. 9, p. 41. (1909)

God will accept the wholehearted service, and will Himself make up the deficiencies. – *The Ministry of Healing*, p. 150. (1905)

Measureless Results Possible. – To everyone who offers himself to the Lord for service, withholding nothing, is given power for the attainment of measureless results. – *Testimonies*, vol. 7, p. 30. (1902)

Accompanied by angels

Ministry of Holy Angels. – We need to understand better than we do the mission of the angels. It would be well to remember that every true child of God has the co-operation of heavenly beings. Invisible armies of light and power attend the meek and lowly ones who believe and claim the promises of God. Cherubim and seraphim, and angels that excel in strength, stand at God's right hand, 'All ministering spirits, sent forth to minister for them who shall be heirs of salvation.' – *The Acts of the Apostles*, p. 154. (1911)

Thousands of Angels. – In working for perishing souls you have the companionship of angels. Thousands upon thousands, and ten thousand times ten thousand angels are waiting to co-operate with members of our churches in communicating the light that God has generously given, that a people may be prepared for the coming of Christ. – *Testimonies*, vol. 9, p. 129. (1909)

They Are Ever Near. – Those who labor for the good of others are working in union with the heavenly angels. They have their constant companionship, their unceasing ministry. Angels of light and power are ever near to

[110]   116

protect, to comfort, to heal, to instruct, to inspire. The highest education, the truest culture, and the most exalted service possible to human beings in this world are theirs. – *Testimonies*, vol. 6, pp. 307, 308. (1900)

Sent to Help Us. – Nothing is apparently more helpless, yet really more invincible, than the soul that feels its nothingness and relies wholly on the merits of the Saviour. God would send every angel in heaven to the aid of such a one, rather than allow him to be overcome. – *Testimonies*, vol. 7, p. 17. (1902)

Our canvassers are having marked success. And why should they not? The heavenly angels are working with them. Hundreds of those who believe the truth will, if they keep their hearts humble, do a good work, in the companionship of heavenly angels. God will use those who humble the heart before him, and sanctify themselves in faith and humility, following the example of the Great Teacher, and speaking words that will enlighten those not of our faith. We are to work patiently and disinterestedly, as the servants of the Lord, opening the Scriptures to others. – *Letter 102,* 1910.

Angels Give Words. – Much responsibility rests upon the canvasser. He should go to his work prepared to explain the Scriptures. If he puts his trust in the Lord as he travels from place to place, angels of God will be round about him, giving him words to speak that will bring light and hope and courage to many souls. – *Testimonies*, vol. 6, p. 314. (1900)

They Come to Soften Hearts. – God will impress those whose hearts are open to truth, and who are longing for guidance. He will say to His human agent, 'Speak to this one or to that one of the love of Jesus.' No sooner is the name of Jesus mentioned in love and tenderness than angels of God draw near, to soften and subdue the heart. – *Manual for Canvassers*, p. 37. (1902)

They Give Instruction. – Every canvasser has positive and constant need of the angelic ministration; for he has an important work to do, a work that he cannot do in his own strength. Those who are born again, who are willing to be guided by the Holy Spirit, doing in Christ's way that which they can do, those who will work as if they could see the heavenly universe watching them, will be accompanied and instructed by holy angels, who will go before them to the dwellings of the people, preparing the way for them. Such help is far above all the advantages which expensive embellishments are supposed to give.

They Give Success. – When men realize the times in which we are living, they will work as in the sight of heaven. The canvasser will handle those books that bring light and strength to the soul. He will drink in the spirit of those books and will put his whole soul into the work of presenting them to the people. His strength, his courage, his success, will depend on how fully the truth presented in the books is woven into his own experience and developed in his character. When his own life is thus molded, he can go forward, representing to others the sacred truth he is handling. Imbued with the Spirit of God he will gain a deep, rich experience, and heavenly angels will give him success in the work. – *Testimonies*, vol. 6, pp. 319, 320. (1900)

Jesus and holy angels will give success to the efforts of intelligent, God-fearing men who do all in their power to save souls. Quietly, modestly, with a heart overflowing with love, let them seek to win minds to investigate the truth, engaging in Bible readings when they can. By so doing they will be sowing the seed of truth beside all waters, showing forth the praises of Him who hath called them out of darkness into His marvelous light. Those who are doing this work from right motives are doing an important work of ministering. They will manifest no feeble, undecided character. Their minds are enlarging, their manners are becoming more refined. They should place no bounds to their improvement, but every day be better fitted to do good work. – *Testimonies*, vol. 5, p. 403. (1885)

CHAPTER 18

Help for every difficulty

A Thousand Ways. – Our heavenly Father has a thousand ways to provide for us of which we know nothing. Those who accept the one principle of making the service of God supreme, will find perplexities vanish, and a plain path before their feet. – *The Ministry of Healing*, p. 481. (1905)

Results Not Measured by Apparent Success. – We are to be sincere, earnest Christians, doing faithfully the duties placed in our hands, and looking ever to Jesus, the Author and Finisher of our faith. Our reward is not dependent upon our seeming success, but upon the spirit in which our work is done. As canvassers or evangelists, you may not have had the success you prayed for, but remember that you do not know and cannot measure the result of faithful effort. – *Manuscript 20*, 1905.

No Need for Discouragement. – When there is a continual reliance upon God, a continual practice of self-denial, the workers will not sink into discouragement. They will not worry. They will remember that in every place there are souls of whom the Lord has need, and whom the devil is seeking, that he may bind them fast in the slavery of sin, of disregard for the law of God. – *Manual for Canvassers*, pp. 22, 23. (1902)

Victory Will Be Given. – The canvasser need not be discouraged if he is called to encounter difficulties in his work; let him work in faith, and victory will be given. 'We wrestle not against flesh and blood, but against principalities, against powers, against the rulers of the darkness of this world.' Whenever a book is presented that will expose error, Satan is close by the side of the one to whom it is offered, and urges reasons why it should not be accepted. But a divine agency is at work to influence minds in favor of the light. Ministering angels will oppose their power to that of Satan. And when through the influence of the Holy Spirit the truth is received into the mind and heart, it will have a transforming power upon the character. – *Manuscript 31*, 1890.

Look Heavenward in Faith. – Take the word of Christ as your assurance. Has He not invited you to come unto Him? Never allow yourself to talk in a hopeless, discouraged way. If you do, you will lose much. By looking at appearances, and complaining when difficulties and pressure come, you give evidence of a sickly, enfeebled faith. Talk and act as if your faith was invincible. The Lord is rich in resources; He owns the world. Look heavenward in faith. Look to Him who has light and power and efficiency. – *Christ's Object Lessons*, pp. 146, 147. (1900)

Believe God's Promise. – Those who work for God will meet with discouragement, but the promise is always theirs: 'Lo, I am with you alway, even unto the end of the world.' Matthew 28:20. God will give a most wonderful experience to those who will say: 'I believe Thy promise; I will not fail nor become discouraged.' – *Testimonies*, vol. 6, pp. 335, 336. (1900)

The Saviour Will Send Help. – The precious Saviour will send help just when we need it. The way to heaven is consecrated by His footprints. Every thorn that wounds our feet has wounded His. Every cross that we are called to bear, He has borne before us. The Lord permits conflicts, to prepare the soul for peace. – *The Great Controversy*, p. 633. (1888)

He Uplifts the Distressed. – Not a sigh is breathed, not a pain felt, not a grief pierces the soul, but the throb vibrates to the Father's heart. . . . God is bending from His throne to hear the cry of the oppressed. To every sincere prayer He answers, 'Here am I.' He uplifts the distressed and downtrodden. In all our afflictions He is afflicted. In every temptation and every trial the Angel of His presence is near to deliver. – *The Desire of Ages*, p. 356. (1898)

Danger of Hesitating and Doubting. – As the prophet [Jonah] thought of the difficulties and seeming impossibilities of this commission, he was tempted to question the wisdom of the call. . . . While he hesitated, still doubting, Satan overwhelmed him with discouragement. . . . In the charge given him, Jonah had been entrusted with a heavy responsibility; yet He who had bidden him go was able to sustain His servant and grant him success. – *Prophets and Kings*, p. 266. (1916)

Let Courage Fail Not. – Never let your courage fail. Never talk unbelief because appearances are against you. As you work for the Master you will feel pressure for want of means, but the Lord will hear and answer your petitions for help. Let your language be: 'The Lord GOD will help me; therefore shall I not be confounded: therefore have I set my face like a flint, and I *know* that I shall not be ashamed.' Isaiah 50:7 [emphasis supplied]. – *Testimonies*, vol. 7, p. 244. (1902)

Let us be hopeful and courageous. Despondency in God's service is sinful and unreasonable. He knows our every necessity. He has all power. He can bestow upon His servants the measure of efficiency that their need demands. – *Testimonies*, vol. 8, p. 38. (1904)

Be strong, and talk hope. Press your way through obstacles. You are in spiritual wedlock with Jesus Christ. The word is your assurance. Approach your Saviour with the full confidence of living faith, joining your hands with His. Go where He leads the way. Whatsoever He says to you, do. He will teach you just as willingly as He will teach someone else. – *Testimonies*, vol. 6, p. 462. (1900)

Exercise Faith of Caleb. – It was Caleb's faith in God that gave him courage; that kept him from the fear of man, even the mighty giants, the sons of Anak, and enabled him to stand boldly and unflinchingly in defense of the right. From the same exalted source, the mighty General of the armies of heaven, every true soldier of the cross of Christ must receive strength and courage to overcome obstacles that often seem insurmountable . . . We want Calebs now . . . who with courageous words will make a strong report in favor of immediate action. – *Testimonies*, vol. 5, pp. 378-383. (1885)

Work With Determination. – Those in the service of God must show animation and determination in the work of winning souls. Remember that there are those who will perish unless we as God's instrumentalities work with a determination that will not fail nor become discouraged. The throne of grace is to be our continual dependence. – *Testimonies*, vol. 6, p. 418. (1900)

Face Difficulties Bravely. – Difficulties will arise that will try your faith and patience. Face them bravely. Look on the bright side. If the work is hindered, be sure that it is not your fault, and then go forward, rejoicing in the Lord. – *Testimonies*, vol. 7, p. 244. (1902)

Trials Mean Benefit. – But when tribulation comes upon us, how many of us are like Jacob! We think it the hand of an enemy; and in the darkness we wrestle blindly until our strength is spent, and we find no comfort or deliverance. . . . We also need to learn that trials mean benefit, and not to despise the chastening of the Lord, nor faint when we are rebuked of Him. – *Thoughts From the Mount of Blessing*, p. 25. (1896)

The Lord Jesus Our Efficiency. – Workers for Christ are never to think, much less to speak, of failure in their work. The Lord Jesus is our efficiency in all things; His Spirit is to be our inspiration; and as we place ourselves in His hands, to be channels of light, our means of doing good will never be exhausted. We may draw upon His fullness, and receive of that grace which has no limit. – *Gospel Workers*, p. 19. (1915)

Expect Great Things. – It is not the capabilities you now possess, or ever will have, that will give you success. It is that which the Lord can do for you. We need to have far less confidence in what man can do, and far more confidence in what God can do for every believing soul. He longs to have you reach after Him by faith. He longs to have you expect great things from Him. He longs to give you understanding in temporal as well as in spiritual matters. He can sharpen the intellect. He can give tact and skill. Put your talents into the work, ask God for wisdom, and it will be given you. – *Christ's Object Lessons*, p. 146. (1900)

All Difficulties Removed. – If you will seek the Lord and be converted every day; if you will of your own spiritual choice be free and joyous in God; if with gladsome consent of heart to His gracious call, you come wearing the yoke of Christ, – the yoke of obedience and service, – all your murmurings will be stilled, all your difficulties will be removed, all the perplexing problems that now confront you will be solved. – *Thoughts From the Mount of Blessing*, p. 101. (1896)

Through most wonderful workings of divine providence, mountains of difficulty will be removed and cast into the sea. – *Testimonies*, vol. 9, p. 96. (1909)

Our truth-filled literature

CHAPTER 19

Books that give the message

Proclaim the Third Angel's Message. – The Lord calls for workers to enter the canvassing field that the books containing the light of present truth may be circulated. The people in the world need to know that the signs of the times are fulfilling. Take to them the books that will enlighten them. . . .

Those who have been long in the truth are asleep. They need to be sanctified by the Holy Spirit. The third angel's message is to be proclaimed with a loud voice. Tremendous issues are before us. We have no time to lose. God forbid that we should allow minor matters to eclipse the light which should be given to the world.

The warning message is to be carried to all parts of the world. Our books are to be published in many different languages. With these books, humble, faithful men are to go forth as colporteur evangelists, bearing the truth to many who otherwise would never be enlightened. – *Manuscript 76, 1901.*

A Definite Mission. – My heart aches as I see those who profess to be looking for the Saviour devoting their time and talents to circulating books that contain nothing concerning the special truths for this time – books of narrative, books of biography, books of men's theories and speculations. The world is full of such books; they can be had anywhere; but how can the followers of Christ engage in so common a work, when there is crying need for God's truth on every hand? It is not our mission to circulate such works. There are thousands of others to do this, who as yet have not sufficient knowledge of anything better. We have a definite mission, and we should not turn from it to side issues. Men and means are not to be employed in bringing before the people books that have no bearing upon the present truth. – *Manual for Canvassers,* p. 51. (1902)

Unless care is taken, the market will be flooded with books of a cheap order, and the people will be deprived of the light and truth which it is essential they should have to prepare the way of the Lord. – *Letter 43,* 1899.

Handle Books That Bring Light to the Soul. – Let canvassers handle books which bring light and strength to the soul, and let them drink in the spirit of these books. Let them put their whole soul into the work of presenting these books to the people. If they are imbued with the Spirit of God, heavenly angels will give them success in their work, and they will gain a deep, rich experience. – *Letter 75,* 1900.

Teach the Evidences of Our Faith. – Our workers should now be encouraged to give their first attention to books that deal with the evidences of our faith – books that teach the doctrines of the Bible and that will prepare a people to stand in the trying times before us. Having brought a people to the enlightenment of the truth by prayerful labor in Bible instruction, and through a wise use of our publications, we are to teach them to become laborers in word and doctrine. We are to encourage them to scatter the books that deal with Bible subjects – books the teachings of which will prepare a people to stand, having their loins girded with truth and their lamps burning. – *Testimonies,* vol. 9, p. 61. (1909)

Contain Present Truth. – Canvassers should be encouraged to take hold of this work, not to canvass for story-books, but to bring before the world the books containing truth essential for this time. – *Testimonies,* vol. 6, p. 315. (1900)

Give the Testing Truths. – The larger books . . . contain present truth for this time – truth that is to be proclaimed in all parts of the world. Our canvassers are to circulate the books that give definite instruction regarding the testing messages that are to prepare a people to stand on the platform of eternal truth, holding aloft the banner on which is inscribed, 'The commandments of God, and the faith of Jesus.'

I have been instructed that the canvassing work is to be revived. Our smaller books, with our pamphlets and journals, can and should be used in connection with our larger books. – *Manuscript 136, 1903.*

CHAPTER 20

Our large message books

Books That Reveal Light on Satan's Apostasy. – *Instruction has been given me that the important books containing the light that God has given regarding Satan's apostasy in heaven should be given a wide circulation just now; for through them the truth will reach many minds. *Patriarchs and Prophets, Daniel and the Revelation,* and *The Great Controversy* are needed now as never before. They should be widely circulated because the truths they emphasize will open many blind eyes. . . . Many of our people have been blind to the importance of the very books that were most needed. Had tact and skill then been shown in the sale of these books, the Sunday-law movement would not be where it is today. – *Review and Herald,* Feb. 16, 1905.

In *The Desire of Ages, Patriarchs and Prophets, The Great Controversy,* and in *Daniel and the Revelation,* there is precious instruction. These books must be regarded as of special importance, and every effort should be made to get them before the people. – *Letter 229,* 1903.

The light given was that *Thoughts on Daniel and the Revelation, The Great Controversy,* and *Patriarchs and*

*NOTE: the reader must keep in mind that, since these statements were penned, a number of large message-filled books have been published and are available to our colporteurs. – compilers.

Prophets, would make their way. They contain the very message the people must have, the special light God had given His people. The angels of God would prepare the way for these books in the hearts of the people. – *Special Instruction Regarding Royalties,* p. 7. (1899)

The Spirit of Prophecy Books. – I thank my heavenly Father for the interest that my brethren and sisters have taken in the circulation of *Christ's Object Lessons*. By the sale of this book great good has been accomplished, and the work should be continued. But the efforts of our people should not be confined to this one book. The work of the Lord includes more than one line of service. *Christ's Object Lessons* is to live and do its appointed work, but not all the thought and effort of God's people are to be given to its circulation. The larger books, *Patriarchs and Prophets, The Great Controversy,* and *The Desire of Ages,* should be sold everywhere. These books contain truth for this time, – truth that is to be proclaimed in all parts of the world. Nothing is to hinder their sale.

The effort to circulate *Christ's Object Lessons* has demonstrated what can be done in the canvassing field. This effort is a never-to-be-forgotten lesson on how to canvass in the prayerful, trustful way that brings success.

Many more of our larger books might have been sold if church members had been awake to the importance of the truths these books contain, and had realized their responsibility to circulate them. My brethren and sisters, will you not now make an effort to circulate these books? and will you not bring into this effort the enthusiasm that you brought into the effort to sell *Christ's Object Lessons?*

In selling this book many have learned how to handle the larger books. They have obtained an experience that has prepared them to enter the canvassing field.

Influence of These Books. – Sister White is not the originator of these books. They contain the instruction that during her lifework God has been giving her. They contain the precious, comforting light that God has graciously given His servant to be given to the world. From their pages this light is to shine into the hearts of men and women, leading them to the Saviour. The Lord has declared that these books are to be scattered throughout the world. There is in them truth which to the receiver is a savor of life unto life. They are silent witnesses for God. In the past they have been the means in His hands of convicting and converting many souls. Many have read them with eager expectation, and, by reading them, have been led to see the efficacy of Christ's atonement, and to trust in its power. They have been led to commit the keeping of their souls to their Creator, waiting and hoping for the coming of the Saviour to take His loved ones to their eternal home. In the future, these books are to make the gospel plain to many others, revealing to them the way of salvation. – *Review and Herald,* Jan. 20, 1903.

Sell Books That Give Light. – The Lord has sent His people much instruction, line upon line, precept upon precept, here a little, and there a little. Little heed is given to the Bible, and the Lord has given a lesser light to lead men and women to the greater light. Oh, how much good would be accomplished if the books containing this light were read with a determination to carry out the principles they contain! There would be a thousandfold greater vigilance, a thousandfold more self-denial and resolute effort. And many more would now be rejoicing in the light of present truth.

My brethren and sisters, work earnestly to circulate these books. Put your hearts into this work, and the blessing of God will be with you. Go forth in faith, praying that God will prepare hearts to receive the light. Be pleasant and courteous. Show by a consistent course that you are true Christians. Walk and work in the light of heaven, and your path will be as the path of the just, shining more and more unto the perfect day. – *Review and Herald,* Jan. 20, 1903.

Truths Barricaded by a 'Thus Saith the Lord.' – How many have read carefully *Patriarchs and Prophets, The Great Controversy,* and *The Desire of Ages?* I wish all to understand that my confidence in the light that God has given stands firm, because I know that the Holy Spirit's power magnified the truth, and made it honorable, saying: 'This is the way, walk ye in it.' In my books, the truth is stated, barricaded by a 'Thus saith the Lord.' The Holy Spirit traced these truths upon my heart and mind as indelibly as the law was traced by the finger of God, upon the tables of stone, which are now in the ark, to be brought forth in that great day when sentence will be pronounced against every evil, seducing science produced by the father of lies. – *Letter 90,* 1906.

God would be pleased to see *The Desire of Ages* in every home. In this book is contained the light He has given upon His word. To our canvassers I would say, Go forth with your hearts softened and subdued by reading of the life of Christ. Drink deeply of the water of salvation, that it may be in your heart as a living spring, flowing forth to refresh souls ready to perish. – *Letter 75, 1900.*

'The Great Controversy,' Above Silver or Gold. – *The Great Controversy* should be very widely circulated. It contains the story of the past, the present, and the future. In its outline of the closing scenes of this earth's history, it bears a powerful testimony in behalf of the truth. I am more anxious to see a wide circulation for this book than for any others I have written; for in *The Great Controversy,* the last message of warning to the world is given more distinctly than in any of my other books. – *Letter 281, 1905.*

I speak to you who are engaged in the canvassing work. Have you read volume 4 [*The Great Controversy*]? Do you know what it contains? Have you any appreciation of the subject matter? Do you not see that the people need the light therein given? If you have not already done so, I entreat you to read carefully these solemn warnings and appeals. I am sure that the Lord would have this work carried into all the highways and byways, where are souls to be warned of the danger so soon to come. – *Letter 1, 1890.*

I was moved by the Spirit of the Lord to write that book, and while working upon it, I felt a great burden upon my soul. I knew that time was short, that the scenes which are soon to crowd upon us would at the last come very suddenly and swiftly, as represented in the words of Scripture: 'The day of the Lord so cometh as a thief in the night.'

The Lord has set before me matters which are of urgent importance for the present time, and which reach into the future. The words have been spoken in a charge to me, 'Write in a book the things which thou hast seen and heard, and let it go to all the people; for the time is at hand when past history will be repeated.' I have been aroused at one, two, or three o'clock in the morning with some point forcibly impressed upon my mind, as if spoken by the voice of God. . . .

I was shown . . . that I should devote myself to writing out the important matters for volume 4 [*The Great Controversy*]; that the warning must go where the living messenger could not go, and that it would call the attention of many to the important events to occur in the closing scenes of this world's history. – *Letter 1, 1890.*

The book *The Great Controversy,* I appreciate above silver or gold, and I greatly desire that it shall come before the people. While writing the manuscript of *The Great Controversy*, I was often conscious of the presence of the angels of God. And many times the scenes about which I was writing were presented to me anew in visions of the night, so that they were fresh and vivid in my mind. – *Letter 56, 1911.*

The Greatest Results Future. – The results of the circulation of this book [*The Great Controversy*] are not to be judged by what now appears. By reading it, some souls will be aroused, and will have courage to unite themselves at once with those who keep the commandments of God. But a much larger number who read it will not take their position until they see the very events taking place that are foretold in it. The fulfillment of some of the predictions will inspire faith that others also will come to pass, and when the earth is lightened with the glory of the Lord, in the closing work, many souls will take their position on the commandments of God as the result of this agency. – *Manuscript 31,* 1890.

Books With a Unique Influence. – God gave me the light contained in *The Great Controversy* and *Patriarchs and Prophets* and this light was needed to arouse the people to prepare for the great day of God, which is just before us. These books contain God's direct appeal to the people. Thus He is speaking to the people in stirring words, urging them to make ready for His coming. The light God has given in these books should not be concealed. . . .

I know that the statement made that these books cannot be sold, is untrue. I know; for the Lord has instructed me that this is said because human devising has blocked the way for their sale. It cannot be denied that these works were not the product of any human mind; they are the voice of God speaking to His people and they will have an influence upon minds that other books do not have. – *Manuscript 23,* 1890.

Many will depart from the faith and give heed to seducing spirits. *Patriarchs and Prophets* and *The Great Controversy,* are books that are especially adapted to those who have newly come to the faith, that they may be established in the truth. The dangers are pointed out that should be avoided by the churches. Those who become thoroughly acquainted with the lessons in these books will see the dangers before them, and will be able to discern the plain, straight path marked out for them. They will be kept from strange paths. They will make straight paths for their feet, lest the lame be turned out of the way. – *Letter 229,* 1903.

Will Preserve From Error. – Let there be an interest awakened in the sale of these books. Their sale is essential; for they contain timely instruction from the Lord. They should be appreciated as books that bring to the people light that is especially needed just now. Therefore these books should be widely distributed. Those who make a careful study of the instruction contained in them, and will receive it as from the Lord, will be kept from receiving many of the errors that are being introduced. Those who accept the truths contained in these books will not be led into false paths.

CHAPTER 21

Health publications

Circulation of Health Publications. – The circulation of our health publications is a most important work. It is a work in which all who believe the special truths for this time should have a living interest. God desires that now, as never before, the minds of the people shall be deeply stirred to investigate the great temperance question and the principles underlying true health reform. . . .

Religion and Health. – True religion and the laws of health go hand in hand. It is impossible to work for the salvation of men and women without presenting to them the need of breaking away from sinful gratifications, which destroy the health, debase the soul, and prevent divine truth from impressing the mind. – *Review and Herald,* Nov. 12, 1901.

Health Reform an Entering Wedge. – The gospel of health has able advocates, but their work has been made very hard because so many ministers, presidents of conferences, and others in positions of influence have failed to give the question of health reform its proper attention. They have not recognized it in its relation to the work of the message as the right arm of the body. While very little respect has been shown to this department by many of the people, and by some of the ministers, the Lord has shown His regard for it by giving it abundant prosperity.

When properly conducted, the health work is an entering wedge, making a way for other truths to reach the heart. When the third angel's message is received in its fullness, health reform will be given its place in the councils of the conference, in the work of the church, in the home, at the table, and in all the household arrangements. Then the right arm will serve and protect the body. – *Testimonies,* vol. 6, p. 327. (1900)

Health Literature the Helping Hand of the Gospel. – Our health literature is the helping hand of the gospel, opening the way for the truth to enter and save many souls. I know of nothing which so quickly unlocks hearts as this literature, which, when read and practiced, leads souls to the searching of the Bible for a better understanding of the truth.

Canvassers should bring the health publications to the notice of those they visit, telling them how useful they are in the treatment of disease. – *Manuscript 113,* 1901.

Arrests Attention. – Publications upon health reform will reach many who will not see or read anything upon important Bible subjects. . . . The truth must come to the people upon health reform. This is essential in order to arrest the attention in regard to Bible truth.

God requires that His people shall be temperate in all things. Unless they practice temperance, they will not, cannot, be sanctified through the truth. Their very thoughts and minds become depraved.

Many of those looked upon as hopelessly depraved, will, if properly instructed in regard to their unhealthful practices, be arrested with the truth. Then they may be elevated, ennobled, sanctified, fit vessels for the Master's use. Go with your hands full of proper reading matter, and your heart full of the love of Christ for their souls, reaching them where they are. . . .

Removes Prejudice. – I have been shown that in giving attention to this branch of the work you remove a large amount of prejudice from many minds, that has barred the way to their receiving the truth and reading the publications setting forth the truth which we believe. This matter must not be passed over as nonessential; for nearly every family needs to be stirred up on this question, and their consciences aroused to be doers of the word of God in practicing self-denial of appetite. When you make the people intelligent on the question of health reform, you have prepared the way for them to give attention to the present truth for these last days. Said my guide, 'Educate, educate, educate.' The mind must be enlightened; for the understanding is darkened just as Satan would have it to be, because he can find access through perverted appetite, to debase the soul. . . .

I am informed by my guide, 'All who believe and proclaim the truth should not only practice health reform, but teach it diligently to others.' This will be a strong agency in calling the attention of the unbelieving to consider that if we are intelligent upon this subject in regard to healthful diet and practices, we would be sound on the subjects of Bible doctrine. – *Manuscript 1, 1875.*

The Lord calls for workers to enter the canvassing field. He desires the books upon health reform to be circulated. Much depends upon the question of health reform. – *Manuscript 174, 1899.*

Let young men and young women take our books on healthful living, and go out among the people, doing their utmost to advance the work of health reform. There are many in the world who are anxious to know more in regard to these principles. – *Letter 154a, 1900.*

Great Need for This Light. – The people are in sad need of the light shining from the pages of our health and temperance journals. God desires to use these journals as mediums through which flashes of light shall arrest the attention of the people, and cause them to heed the warning of the message of the third angel. . . .

Ministers can and should do much to urge the circulation of the health journals. Every member of the church should work as earnestly for these journals as for our other periodicals. There should be no friction between the two. . . .

The circulation of the health journals will be a powerful agency in preparing the people to accept those special truths that are to fit them for the soon coming of the Son of man. – *Review and Herald, Nov. 12, 1901.*

A Permanent Part of Our Literature. – Health reform will reach a class and has reached a class that otherwise would never have been reached by the truth. There is a great necessity for labor being put forth to help the people, believers and unbelievers, at the present time by health talks, and health publications. I cannot see why the health books should not have a permanent place as well as the other publications notwithstanding human prejudices to the contrary. – *Letter 25a, 1889.*

CHAPTER 22

Maintaining a proper balance

Health and Religious Books. – Perfect unity should exist among the workers who handle the books that are to flood the world with light. Wherever the canvassing work is presented among our people, let both the health books and the religious books be presented together as parts of a united work. The relation of the religious and the health books is presented to me as illustrated by the union of the warp and the woof to form a beautiful pattern and a perfect piece of work.

Equally Important. – In the past the health books have not been handled with the interest which their importance demands. Though by a large class they have been highly appreciated, yet many have not thought it essential that they should go to the world. But what can be a better preparation for the coming of the Lord and for the reception of other truths essential to prepare a people for His coming than to arouse the people to see the evils of this age and to stir them to reformation from self-indulgent and unhealthful habits? Is not the world in need of being aroused on the subject of health reform? Are not the people in need of the truths presented in the health books? A different sentiment from that which has heretofore prevailed regarding the health works should be entertained by many of our canvassers in the field.

Divisions and distinct parties should not be seen among our canvassers and general agents [publishing department secretaries]. All should be interested in the sale of the books treating upon the health question as well as in the sale of the distinctively religious works. The line is not to be drawn that certain books only are to occupy the attention of the canvassers. There must be perfect unity, a well-balanced, symmetrical development of the work in all its parts.

Not to Be Separated. – The indifference with which the health books have been treated by many is an offense to God. To separate the health work from the great body of the work is not in His order. Present truth lies in the work of health reform as verily as in other features of gospel work. No one branch when separated from others can be a perfect whole. – *Testimonies,* vol. 6, pp. 326, 327. (1900)

No One Branch a Specialty. – In all our work, caution should be used that no one branch be made a specialty, while other interests are left to suffer. There has not been that interest taken in the circulation of our health journals that there should be. The circulation of these journals must not be neglected, or the people will suffer a great loss. – *Review and Herald,* Nov. 12, 1901.

Each Has Its Proper Place. – But while the health work has its place in the promulgation of the third angel's message, its advocates must not in any way strive to make it take the place of the message. The health books should occupy their proper position, but the circulation of these books is only one of many lines in the great work to be done. The glowing impressions sometimes given to the canvasser in regard to the health books must not result in excluding from the field other important books that should come before the people. Those who have charge of the canvassing work should be men who can discern the relation of each part of the work to the great whole. Let them give due attention to the circulation of the health books, but not make this line so prominent as to draw men away from other lines of vital interest, thus excluding the books that bear the special message of truth to the world.

Just as much education is necessary for the handling of the religious books as for the handling of those treating upon the question of health and temperance. Just as much should be said in regard to the work of canvassing for books containing spiritual food, just as much effort should be made to encourage and educate workers to circulate the books containing the third angel's message, as is said and done to develop workers for the health books.

Each Complements the Other. – The one class of books will always make a place for the other. Both are essential, and both should occupy the field at the same time. Each is the complement of the other and can in no wise take its place. Both treat on subjects of highest value, and both must act their part in the preparation of the people of God for these last days. Both should stand as present truth to enlighten, to arouse, to convince. Both should blend in the work of sanctifying and purifying the churches that are looking and waiting for the coming of the Son of God in power and great glory.

Let each publisher and general agent [publishing department secretary] work enthusiastically to encourage the agents [colporteurs] now in the field and to hunt up and train new workers. Let each strengthen and build up the work as much as possible without weakening the work of others. Let all be done in brotherly love and without selfishness. – *Testimonies,* vol. 6, pp. 327, 328. (1900)

Work to Develop Symmetrically. – The health reform is as closely related to the third angel's message as the arm to the body; but the arm cannot take the place of the body. The proclamation of the third angel's message, the commandments of God and the testimony of Jesus, is the burden of our work. The message is to be proclaimed with a loud cry, and is to go to the whole world. The presentation of health principles must be united with this message, but must not in any case be independent of it, or in any way take the place of it. . . . There must be a well-balanced, symmetrical development of the work in all its parts. . . . I would have the health books occupy their proper place; but they are only one of many lines in the great work to be done. The Lord has sent His message to the world in books that contain the truth for the last days.

Canvassers should not be taught that one book or one class of books is to occupy the field, to the neglect of all others. Among the workers are always some who can be swayed in almost any direction. Those who have charge of the canvassing work should be men of well-balanced minds, who can discern the relation of each part of the work to the great whole. Let them give due attention to the circulation of health books, but not make this line so prominent as to draw men away from other lines of vital interest. – *Letter 57, 1896.*

The sale of health journals and books in no way hinders the sale of the publications dealing with other phases of the third angel's message. All are to prepare the way for the Lord Jesus to come in the clouds of heaven with power and great glory. – *Manuscript 113, 1901.*

Not All to Work for One Book. – It has been urged as the best policy that only one book at a time should have a place in the canvassing field, – that all the canvassers should work for the same book. Could this be done, it would not be wise nor expedient. No one book should be carried exclusively and kept before the public as if it could supply every demand for this time. If the Lord has light for His people, brought out in different ways in various books, who shall venture to put up barriers so that the light shall not be diffused throughout the world? The Lord desires our brethren to devise plans so that the light He has given shall not be hid in our publishing houses, but shall shine forth to enlighten all who will receive it. – *Manual for Canvassers,* p. 47. (1902)

Literature for All Classes. – No canvasser should exalt the book for which he is working above others that set forth the truth for this time. Should our canvassers drop all but one book, and concentrate their energies on that, the work would not be carried on according to God's plan. Minds are not constituted alike, and what might be food for one might fail to attract another; therefore, books should be in the field treating in a variety of ways the special subjects for this time. It will be necessary for the canvasser to make a wise selection. Let no one who is doing the work of God become narrow and shortsighted. The Lord has many instrumentalities through which He designs to work. When one book is exalted above another, there is danger that the very work best adapted to give light to the people will be crowded out. There is no need of contrasting different books, and judging as to which will do the most good. God has a place for all the voices and all the pens that he has inspired to utterance for Him. It will be difficult for some minds to fathom our most difficult works, and a simpler way of putting the truth will reach them more readily. Let the leading workers encourage the weaker ones, and show an equal interest in every one of the instrumentalities set in motion to prepare a people for the day of the Lord. Some would receive more benefit from papers and tracts than from books. Papers, tracts, and pamphlets that dwell upon Bible lessons, all need attention in the canvassing work, for they are as little wedges that open the way for larger works. – *Manual for Canvassers,* pp. 48, 49. (1902)

Tracts and Pamphlets. – The canvasser should carry with him tracts, pamphlets, and small books to give to those who cannot buy. In this way the truth can be introduced into many homes. – *Testimonies,* vol. 6, p. 338. (1900)

More Decided Efforts for Religious Books. – Canvassing for our publications is an important and most profitable evangelistic work. . . . While we have said much in regard to canvassing for the health books, – and we still feel that we should circulate these books, – yet more decided efforts should be made to carry our important religious books to the people. Our publications can go to places where meetings cannot now be held. In such places the faithful evangelistic canvasser takes the place of the living preacher. – *Letter 14,* 1902.

At this period of our work we must guard every step we take in reference to the publication of our books. I have been plainly shown that we must secure as canvassers men and women of ability. Much of the effort that has been devoted to the sale of medical books should now be given to the handling of books that contain the present truth for this time, that the evidences of our faith and the issues that are before us may be known by the people. . . .

We are to bring into the work every living agency who feels that he is chosen of God to do, not a common, commercial work, but a work that will give light and truth, Bible truth, to the world. – *Letter 72,* 1907.

Small Books vs. Large Books. – I do not believe it is right to devote so much attention to the sale of the smaller books, to the neglect of the larger ones. It is wrong to leave lying on the shelves the large works that the Lord has revealed should be put into the hands of the people, and to push so vigorously, in the place of these, the sale of small books. – *Manuscript 123,* 1902.

No Time for the Commonplace. – We are now altogether too near the close of this earth's history to keep before the attention of the people a class of books which do not contain the message which our people need. Draw their attention to books treating on practical faith and godliness. Cleanse and sanctify the camp. There is an abundance of books which will give light to the world.

I cannot understand why our papers should contain so many notices of books unessential for this time. Plenty of such books can be obtained in all bookstores. Why not draw the minds of the people to subjects relating to the words of eternal life? Why not make an effort to obtain communications simple, real, and true, from our workers in all parts of the world? God calls for this class of reading. We have no time to devote to commonplace things, no time to waste on books which only amuse. – *Counsels to Writers and Editors,* pp. 147, 148. (1899)

I have been instructed that the common stories put into book form are not essential to our well-being. The world is flooded with this class of literature, and the fact that such books find a ready sale is by no means evidence that they are the books which should be circulated. The passion of stories is bringing into existence many thousands of worthless books, which are as hay, wood, and stubble. These books are written by those whose minds have been educated to run in a channel of romance. Everything that the imaginative mind can think of is woven into the book, and presented to the world as mental food. But very often it has no food value. 'What is the chaff to the wheat?' We do not need novels; for we are dealing with the stern realities of life. – *Counsels to Writers and Editors,* p. 147. (1899)

Avoid Frivolous and Exciting Literature. – The world is deluged with books that might better be consumed rather than circulated. Books upon Indian warfare and similar topics, published and circulated as a money-making scheme, might better never be read. There is a satanic fascination in these books. The heart-sickening relation of crimes and atrocities has a bewitching power upon many youth, exciting in them the desire to bring themselves into notice, even by the most wicked deeds. There are many works more strictly historical whose influence is little better. The enormities, the cruelties, the licentious practices, portrayed in these writings, have acted as leaven in many minds, leading to the commission of similar acts. Books that delineate the satanic deeds of human beings are giving publicity to evil works. The horrible details of crime and misery need not be lived over, and none who believe the truth for this time should act a part in perpetuating their memory.

Love stories and frivolous and exciting tales constitute another class of books that is a curse to every reader. The author may attach a good moral, and all through his work may weave religious sentiments; yet in most cases Satan is but clothed in angel robes, the more effectually to deceive and allure. The mind is affected in a great degree by that upon which it feeds. The readers of frivolous, exciting tales become unfitted for the duties lying before them. They lead an unreal life, and have no desire for useful employment, and no desire to search the Scriptures, to feed upon the heavenly manna. The mind is enfeebled, and loses its power to contemplate the great problems of duty and destiny.

I have been instructed that the youth are exposed to the greatest peril from improper reading. Satan is constantly leading both the youth and those of mature age to be charmed with worthless stories. Could a large share of the books published be consumed, a plague would be stayed that is doing a fearful work in weakening the mind and corrupting the heart. None are so confirmed in right principles as to be secure from temptation. All this trashy reading should be resolutely discarded.

We have no permission from the Lord to engage in either the printing or the sale of such literature, for it is the means of destroying many souls. I know of what I am writing; for this matter has been opened before me. Let not those who believe the truth engage in this work, thinking to make money. The Lord will put a blight upon the means thus obtained; He will scatter more than is gathered. – *Manual for Canvassers,* pp. 51-53. (1902)

Canvass to Diffuse Light. – In this age the trivial is praised and magnified. There is a call for anything that will create a sensation and make sales. The country is flooded with utterly worthless publications, which were written for the sake of making money, while really valuable books are unsold and unread. Those who handle this sensational literature because by so doing they can make higher wages are missing a precious opportunity to do good. There are battles to be fought to arrest the attention of men and women, and interest them in really valuable books that have the Bible for their foundation; and it will be a still greater task to find conscientious, God-fearing workers who will enter the field to canvass for these books for the purpose of diffusing light. – *Testimonies,* vol. 5, pp. 401, 402. (1885)

CHAPTER 23

Our magazine ministry

Presenting the truth through our periodicals. – Blessed, soul-saving Bible truths are published in our papers. There are many who can help in the work of selling our periodicals. – *Testimonies,* vol. 9, p. 63. (1909)

We have been asleep, as it were, regarding the work that may be accomplished by the circulation of well-prepared literature. Let us now, by the wise use of periodicals and books, preach the word with determined energy, that the world may understand the message that Christ gave to John on the Isle of Patmos. Let every human intelligence who professes the name of Christ testify, The end of all things is at hand; prepare to meet thy God. – *Review and Herald,* July 30, 1908.

Proclaim the Third Angel's Message. – The great and wonderful work of the last gospel message is to be carried on now as it has never been before. The world is to receive the light of truth through an evangelizing ministry of the word in our books and periodicals. Our publications are to show that the end of all things is at hand. I am bidden to say to our publishing houses, Lift up the standard; lift it up higher. Proclaim the third angel's message, that it may be heard by all the world. Let it be seen that 'here are they that keep the commandments of God, and the faith of Jesus.' Let our literature give the message as a witness to all the world. – *Review and Herald,* July 30, 1908.

Periodical Subscriptions. – A mistake has been made in soliciting subscriptions for our periodicals for only a few weeks, when by a proper effort much longer subscriptions might have been obtained. One yearly subscription is of more value than many for a short time. When the paper is taken for only a few months, the interest often ends with the short subscription. Few renew their subscriptions for a longer period, and thus there is a large outlay of time that brings small returns, when, with a little more tact and perseverance, yearly subscriptions might have been obtained. You strike too low, brethren; you are too narrow in your plans. You do not put into your work all the tact and perseverance that it deserves. There are more difficulties in this work than in some other branches of business; but the lessons that will be learned, the tact and discipline that will be acquired, will fit you for other fields of usefulness, where you may minister to souls. Those who poorly learn their lesson, and are careless and abrupt in approaching persons, would show the same defects of manner, the same want of tact and skill in dealing with minds, should they enter the ministry.

Short Subscriptions a Mistake. – While short subscriptions are accepted, some will not make the effort necessary to obtain them for a longer time. Canvassers should not go over the ground in a careless, unconcerned manner. They should feel that they are God's workmen, and the love of souls should lead them to make every effort to enlighten men and women in regard to the truth. Providence and grace, means and ends, are closely connected. When His laborers do the very best they can, God does for them that which they cannot do themselves; but no one need expect to succeed independently and by his own exertions. There must be activity united with firm trust in God.

Economy is needed in every department of the Lord's work. The natural turn of youth in this age is to neglect and despise economy, and to confound it with stinginess and narrowness. But economy is consistent with the most broad and liberal views and feelings; there can be no true generosity where it is not practiced. No one should think it beneath him to study economy and the best means of taking care of the fragments. Said Christ, after He had performed a notable miracle: 'Gather up the fragments that remain, that nothing be lost.' – *Testimonies,* vol. 5, pp. 399, 400. (1885)

CHAPTER 24

The far-reaching influence of our publications

Power of the Pen. – The pen is a power in the hands of men who feel the truth burning upon the altar of their hearts, and who have an intelligent zeal for God, balanced with sound judgment. The pen, dipped in the fountain of pure truth, can send the beams of light to dark corners of the earth, which will reflect its rays back, adding new power, and giving increased light to be scattered everywhere. – *Life Sketches,* p. 214. (1915)

The Press God's Instrumentality. – The press is a powerful means to move the minds and hearts of the people. . . . The press is a powerful instrumentality which God has ordained to be combined with the energies of the living preacher to bring the truth before all nations, kindreds, tongues, and peoples. Many minds can be reached in no other way. – *Christian Experience,* pp. 225-227. (1922)

The publishing branch of our cause has much to do with our power. I do desire that it shall accomplish all that the Lord designs it should. If our bookmen do their part faithfully, I know, from the light God has given me, that the knowledge of present truth will be doubled and trebled. – *Life Sketches,* pp. 446, 447. (1915)

Influence of Our Publications. – I have been shown that our publications should be printed in different languages and sent to every civilized country, at any cost. What is the value of money at this time, in comparison with the value of souls? . . .

I have been shown that the press is powerful for good or evil. This agency can reach and influence the public mind as no other means can. The press, controlled by men who are sanctified to God, can be a power indeed for good in bringing men to the knowledge of the truth. . . .

In Other Lands. – I have been shown that the publications already have been doing a work upon some minds in other countries, in breaking down the walls of prejudice and superstition. I was shown men and women studying with intense interest papers and a few pages of tracts upon present truth. They would read the evidences so wonderful and new to them, and would open their Bibles with a deep and new interest, as subjects of truth that had been dark to them were made plain, especially the light in regard to the Sabbath of the fourth commandment. As they searched the Scriptures to see if these things were so, a new light shone upon their understanding, for angels were hovering over them, and impressing their minds with the truths contained in the publications they had been reading.

Searching With Prayer and Tears. – I saw them holding papers and tracts in one hand, and the Bible in the other, while their cheeks were wet with tears; and bowing before God in earnest, humble prayer, to be guided into all truth, – the very thing He was doing for them before they called upon Him. And when the truth was received in their hearts, and they saw the harmonious chain of truth, the Bible was to them a new book; they hugged it to their hearts with grateful joy, while their countenances were all aglow with happiness and holy joy.

These were not satisfied with merely enjoying the light themselves, and they began to work for others. Some made great sacrifices for the truth's sake and to help those of the brethren who were in darkness. The way is thus preparing to do a great work in the distribution of tracts and papers in other languages. – *Life Sketches,* pp. 214, 215. (1915)

Books Taken From Shelves. – It is true that some who buy the books will lay them on the shelf or place them on the parlor table and seldom look at them. Still God has a care for His truth, and the time will come when these books will be sought for and read. Sickness or misfortune may enter the home, and through the truth contained in the books God sends to troubled hearts peace and hope and rest. His love is revealed to them, and they understand the preciousness of the forgiveness of their sins. Thus the Lord co-operates with His self-denying workers. – *Testimonies,* vol. 6, pp. 313, 314. (1900)

Souls Brought to Christ. – Our publications are now sowing the gospel seed, and are instrumental in bringing as many souls to Christ as the preached word. Whole churches have been raised up as the result of their circulation. – *Review and Herald,* June 10, 1880.

Even the Fragments Are Precious. – We should treat as a sacred treasure every line of printed matter containing present truth. Even the fragments of a pamphlet or of a periodical should be regarded as of value. Who can estimate the influence that a torn page containing the truths of the third angel's message may have upon the heart of some seeker after truth? Let us remember that somebody would be glad to read all the books and papers we can spare. Every page is a ray of light from heaven, to shine into the highways and the hedges, shedding light upon the pathway of truth.

In the miracle of feeding the multitude with a few loaves and fishes, the food was increased as it passed from Christ to those who accepted it. Thus it will be in the distribution of our publications. God's truth, as it is passed out, will multiply greatly. And as the disciples by Christ's direction gathered up the fragments which remained, that nothing should be lost, so we should treasure every fragment of literature containing the truth for this time. – *Review and Herald,* August 27, 1903.

A Thousand in One Day. – God will soon do great things for us if we lie humble and believing at His feet. . . . More than one thousand will soon be converted in one day, most of whom will trace their first convictions to the reading of our publications. – *Review and Herald,* Nov. 10, 1885.

When the Final Warning Is Given. – By thousands of voices, all over the earth, the warning will be given. Miracles will be wrought, the sick will be healed, and signs and wonders will follow the believers. Satan also works with lying wonders, even bringing down fire from heaven in the sight of men. Thus the inhabitants of the earth will be brought to take their stand.

The message will be carried not so much by argument as by the deep conviction of the Spirit of God. The arguments have been presented. The seed has been sown, and now it will spring up and bear fruit. The publications distributed by missionary workers have exerted their influence, yet many whose minds were impressed have been prevented from fully comprehending the truth or from yielding obedience. Now the rays of light penetrate everywhere, the truth is seen in its clearness. . . . A large number take their stand upon the Lord's side. – *The Great Controversy*, p. 612. (1888)

God's Plan for Proclaiming the Message. – To us as a people God has given great light, and He calls upon us to let it shine forth to those in darkness. By us the light, the power, of a living truth is to be given to the world. From us there is to shine forth to those in darkness a clear, steady light, kept alive by the power of God. We are charged to use the light given us to create other lights, that our fellow men may rejoice in the truth. Let us not disregard the charge. Suppose that the sun should refuse to shine, what terrible darkness and confusion would result! For us to refuse to let our light shine to those in darkness is to contract guilt, the magnitude of which cannot be computed. . . .

'The Spirit and the bride say, Come. And let him that heareth say, Come. And let him that is athirst come. And whosoever will, let him take the water of life freely.'

These words outline God's plan for the promulgation of the gospel. His instrumentalities, divine and human, are to unite in an effort to save the lost. These souls are to be rescued from the bondage of sin. God calls upon those who have taken His name to obey His orders. All are called to take some part in His work. . . .

Transforming Power of Truth. – It is through the transforming influence of divine grace on human hearts that the power of the word of truth is revealed. The message, proclaimed in regions where it has not yet been heard, makes an impression on hearts. It seems to have greater power in transforming character than when presented to those who are familiar with its office work. Truth has little power on the hearts of those who walk contrary to it for advantage to themselves – those who follow a course opposed to its principles. Such ones profess to believe the word of God, but they give no evidence that they are sanctified by it.

The truth is to take possession of the will of those who have never before heard it. They will see the sinfulness of sin, and their repentance will be thorough and sincere. The Lord will work upon hearts that in the past have not been appealed to, hearts that heretofore have not seen the enormity of sin.

Christ is the only successful antagonist that sin has ever encountered. Let the full light of His life stream into the souls of those who are in darkness. Under the direct power of the gospel thousands have been converted in a day.

When a sinner becomes sensible of the fact that only through Christ can he gain eternal life; when he realizes that obedience to God's word is the condition of entrance into the kingdom of God; when he sees Christ as the propitiation for sin, he comes to the Saviour in humility and contrition, confessing his sins and seeking forgiveness. His soul is impressed with a sense of the majesty and glory of God. The blessedness of an eternal life of peace and joy and purity is felt so deeply that an entire surrender is made.

I am instructed to say that some who outwardly appear the most fully given to sin will, when light flashes into the soul, make most successful workers in places where there are just such sinners as they themselves once were.

Written for Canvassers. – I write this because those engaged in canvassing work and in house-to-house labor often meet men and women who are coarse and forbidding in outward appearance, but who, if won to the truth, will be among its most loyal and stanch adherents. The spirit of truth is indeed of value in any church. Those whom the Lord uses may not always have outward polish, but if they have integrity of character, the Lord accounts them precious.

God's Work to Increase as End Draws Near. – As the end draws near, the work of God is to increase in full strength and purity and holiness. The workers are to be filled with love for God and for one another. They are to cherish principles of the strictest integrity. When the true keynote is struck, God will reveal Himself as a God of mercy and love. Angels of heaven will draw near to the members of the church on earth to aid them in their necessity. Let us ever remember that we are laborers together with God. In this heavenly union we shall carry forward His work with completeness, with singing and rejoicing. In every soul will be kindled the fire of holy zeal. Company after company will leave the dark standard of the foe to come up to the help of the Lord, to the help of the Lord against the mighty.

Workers Must Gain Deeper Experience. – God's workers must gain a far deeper experience. If they will surrender all to Him, He will work mightily for them. They will plant the standard of truth upon fortresses till then held by Satan, and with shouts of victory take possession of them. They bear the scars of battle, but there comes to them the comforting message that the Lord will lead them on, conquering and to conquer.

When God's servants with consecrated zeal co-operate with divine instrumentalities, the state of things that exists in this world will be changed, and soon the earth will with joy receive her King. Then 'they that be wise shall shine as the brightness of the firmament; and they that turn many to righteousness as the stars for ever and ever.' – *Review and Herald,* Sept. 17, 1903.

The colporteur's reward

When the redeemed stand before God, precious souls will respond to their names who are there because of the faithful, patient efforts put forth in their behalf, the entreaties and earnest persuasions to flee to the Stronghold. Thus those who in this world have been laborers together with God will receive their reward.[1]

What will be the gratitude of souls that will meet us in the heavenly courts as they understand the sympathetic, loving interest which has been taken in their salvation! All praise, honor, and glory will be given to God and to the Lamb for our redemption; but it will not detract from the glory of God to express gratitude to the instrumentality He has employed in the salvation of souls ready to perish.

The redeemed will meet and recognize those whose attention they have directed to the uplifted Saviour. What blessed converse they have with these souls! 'I was a sinner,' it will be said, 'without God and without hope in the world, and you came to me, and drew my attention to the precious Saviour as my only hope.' . . .

What rejoicing there will be as these redeemed ones meet and greet those who have had a burden in their behalf![2]

---

[1]*Testimonies for the Church*, vol. 8, pages 196, 197.
[2]*ibid* vol. 6, pages 310-312.

Scripture Index
General Index

Scripture Index

General Index

All figures in index represent actual page numbers; for page numbers in the first edition of *Colporteur Ministry*, see figures in square brackets at the bottom of each page.